NEWSPAPER AND MEDIA TERMINOLOGIES

NEWSPAPER AND MEDIA TERMINOLOGIES

By

K.c. Thakur

2008

CYBER TECH PUBLICATIONS
4264/3, Ansari Road, Daryaganj, New Delhi-110002 (India)
Ph.: 011-23244078. Fax: 011-23280028
E-Mail: cyberpublicationsdelhi@yahoo.com

NEWSPAPER AND MEDIA TERMINOLOGIES

K.C. Thakur

First Edition 2008

Reprint 2024

Published by :

G.S. Rawat for **Cyber Tech Publications**
4264/3, Ansari Road, Daryaganj, New Delhi-110002 (India)
Ph.: 011-23244078. Fax: 011-23280028
E-Mail: cyberpublicationsdelhi@yahoo.com

Printed at : **Amit Enterprises**, Maujpur, Delhi, (9810878184)

Preface

In the developing world every thing is going with a rapid pace. Media is one of the fastest growing sectors. Everyday a few new technologies are being added to it. The working area of the media is also growing or we can say whole world is under its flag. As with the development a few new words and terminologies are also being come to be used in it. The terminologies of Media and Newspaper are not as is used in our everyday life, rather they are very different. The students and readers or the people involved in it must be acquainted with these terminologies. But they have difficulties in getting acquainted with them. Author has felt this cleavage and endeavoured to work for the same. Preseant book is result of the same. Here author has researched over every possible term and put them in alphabetical form for easy reference category-wise.

This book can be used as a ready to refer tool by the students and media persons.

It is sincere hope of the undersigned that this book will be really a dictionary of journalism and media terms. If it could serve a little of its purpose the efforts put by the author in writing this book will be amply rewarded.

—Author

Contents

Preface

Newspapers and Journalism	1
List of Broadcasting Terms	2
Newspaper Vocabulary	24
Journalism Glossary	28
A Glossary of Important Concepts	47
Glossary of Journalism Terms	62
Journalism Terms	64
Glossary of Newspaper Terms	70
Glossary of Newspaper Terms	101
Newspaper Glossary	105
Glossary of Common Newspaper Terms	109
Film Editing Glossary	120
Vocabulary	141
Effects Research: Glossary	150
Theories of Mass Communication	191
A Glossary of Media Literacy Terms	201
General Media Terms	212
Internet Media Terms	218
Out-of-Home Terms	241
Print Media Terms	242

NEWSPAPERS AND JOURNALISM

Article	:	A text or piece of writing on any non-fiction subject.
Broadsheet U.K.	:	A large-format newspaper with usually serious contents.
Censor	:	Official with the power to stop publication of certain articles - censorship n.
Chequebook journalism	:	The obtaining of exclusive rights to a story by payment of large sums of money.
Correspondent	:	1. Person who writes a letter to a paper. 2. Person who writes articles for a paper.
Critic	:	A person who writes articles, esp. stating opinion, about art, music etc.
Desk	:	A department of a newspaper [eg: the sports desk].
Edit	:	To check, modify and generally prepare written material for publication.
Editor	:	1. A person who edits. 2. The head of a newspaper or newspaper department.
Editorial	:	An article written by the editor stating his opinion.
Exclusive rights	:	Rights or permission for one paper to publish a story that no other paper can.

Feature : A special or regular article in a newspaper, usually displayed prominently.

Front page : The first page of a paper, usually carrying the most important story.

Headline : 1. The title at the top of an article.

2. Headlines the most important stories.

Journalist : A person employed to write articles for a newspaper - journalism n.

Media : The media all the means of mass communication (papers, TV, radio etc.).

Opinion : What a person thinks about a particular subject; a subjective point of view.

Paper : 1. Thin, flexible material for writing or printing on.

2. Newspaper.

Story : A news article or report

Tabloid : A small-format paper, with short, sensational stories - see broadsheet

LIST OF BROADCASTING TERMS

With every new technology a number of terms and slang words develop to assist in the rapid communication of ideas between the users of the technology.

Below is a glossary of terms used in broadcasting.

ABC : In the US, American Broadcasting Company, a television and radio network originally created out of NBC. In Australia, the Australian Broadcasting Corporation. In the UK, ABC Weekend TV, a former ITV broadcaster.

A/D : Analog-to-digital conversion.

Absolute Event : A scheduled event whose start time is determined with an assigned time based upon the facility master clock.

Access Time : The total time required to find, retrieve and commence using information, also known as Lead Time.

Actives : Listeners who contact the radio show regarding requests, contests or other interaction.

ADC : Analog to Digital Converter. A device to convert analog signals to digital.

Aircheck : The recorded copy of a broadcast. This can be a digital or analog recording.

Analog Recording : Recording of audio using an electronic signal that varies continuously. The main drawback of analog recording is the introduction of inherent noise to the recorded signal.

Analog Transmission : The broadcasting of a signal using an analog recording. Examples of use include radio.

Arbitron : The company that provides the Industry accepted standard for audience measurement.

Artifacts : Noticeable loss of video and/or audio fidelity in a broadcast or recording caused by limitations in the technology used. Usually reflects undesirable distortion(s) of the original when digitized.

Aspect ratio : The ratio between the width and the height of the picture. In 'traditional' television sets, this is 4:3; in widescreen sets, 16:9. Sometimes printed decimally as 1.33:1 for 4:3 and 1.78:1 for 16:9.

Aston : An on-screen overlayed graphic, usually giving the name of the speaker or reporter in vision.

ATR : Audio Tape Recorder.

A method of recording sound by electromagnetic pulses on a sensitised plastic strip.

ATSC : Advanced Television Systems Committee.

A committee established by the FCC to decide the technical standards for digital broadcasting in the US.

Average Quarter : The term used in audience

Hour @measurement by Arbitron. It is defined às the number of persons listening to a particular station for at least five minutes during a quarter hour. Typical audience measurements may be in the order of ten thousand for the larger shows. (eg Jerry Springer scored 1,600 in the 12+ age group in the spring 2005 figures. Rush Limbaugh scored 16,400 in the same report)

Backcell : The technique where the DJ announces the song title and/or artist of the song that has just played. Also known as "back announcing".

Backtiming : Where the DJ calculates the intro time on the song in an attempt to talk over the intro of the song and finish just prior to the vocals commencing.

Bandwidth : The available space between two given points on the electro-magnetic spectrum and, inter alia, the amount of information that can be squeezed into that space.

BBC : British Broadcasting Corporation.

The main public service broadcaster in the United Kingdom, founded as the British Broadcasting Company in 1922.

Bed : A production element, usually instrumental music or sound effect played in the background of a spoken commercial, promo or other announcement.

Bel : A measure of voltage, current or power gain. One Bel is defined as a tenfold increase in power. If an amplifier increases a signal's power by a factor of 10, its power gain is 1 Bel or 10 decibels (dB). If power is increased by 100 times, the power gain is 2 Bels or 20 decibels. 0.3dB is considered doubling.

Bias : A constant amplitude high frequency signal added to the recording signal to improve the signal to noise ratio and reduce the distortion of an analog tape recording.

Billboard : A short announcement to identify a sponsor at the beginning or end of a production element such as the news or traffic/weather reports.

Book : A slang term for the Arbitron rating period.

Breakbumper : An animation or logotype briefly shown after the end of a programme or part of a programme before the advertising. See also "optical".

Bug : Slang term for a DOG (Digitally Originated Graphic) permanent on screen logo.

Bumper or Bumper Music : A pre-recorded production element containing voice over music that acts as a transition to or from a stop set and other content.

Call Letters : The official name of the radio station in the USA. Also known as a station's callsign.

Cans : Slang for headphones.

CBS : Columbia Broadcasting System, an American television and radio network.

CCIR : Comité consultatif international pour la radio.

In English, "International Radio Consultative Committee", the organisation responsible for assigning requencies to radio stations between 1927 and 1992. Now known as ITU-R.

Closed Captioning : Text version of a programme's dialogue, overlayed on the screen by an equipped television set for the hearing impaired.

Clutter : An excessive number of non-programme elements (such as commercials) appearing one after another.

Copy : The written material used in producing a PSA, promo, or commercial that is meant to be read out by the DJ or presenter.

Crash : When an announcement, jingle or graphic overlaps with a fixed point in the schedule (eg the news or a time signal), usually due to poor timing.

Crossfade : The technique where a DJ, producer or engineer fades out the out going track at the same time as fading in the new track.

Coverage : Percentage of households that can tune into a radio station within the theoretical broadcast radius.

Cueing : Whilst the previous record was playing the DJ would attempt to find the beginning of the song on the next record. The DJ would place the needle down in approximately the right area then move the record back and forth Cueing on the turntable until the beginning of the song was found. When the previous song completed playing the DJ would introduce the next song and turn the record deck on and the record would quickly whirl up to speed with a characteristic distortion. This was later minimised by the use of a slip mat.

Cue Burn : Cue burn relates to the days of vinyl records (33rpm , 45rpm). Whilst the previous record was playing the DJ would attempt to find the beginning of the song on the next record. The DJ would place the needle down in approximately the right area then move the record back and forth Cueing on the turntable until the beginning of the song was found. This cueing back and forth would rub the vinyl and damage the records creating a characteristic noise.

Cue dot : A small square inserted in the corner of the picture to inform rebroadcasters that an advertisement break is about to happen. In the UK, this appeared exactly one minute before the break and disappeared 55 seconds later.

Cume : Short for cumulative audience. A similar term of measurement to a newspaper or magazines' circulation figures.

DAB : Digital Audio Broadcasting.

The use of digital encoding to send higher quality or a greater number of radio services to equipped receivers.

DAC : Digital to Analog Converter . Equipment that changes digital signals into pictures or sound.

Daypart : The radio station's broadcast day is normally split up (starting at 6am) into a series of 4 hour sessions containing one or more shows.

DB or Decibel : One tenth of a bel. See also Bel.

DBS : Direct Broadcasting (by) Satellite

Television and radio programmes distributed by satellite for reception via a dish at the receiver's property.

Dead air : The time on-air where there is no audible transmission. This silence can be down to any of the following:

* DJ, Producer or Engineer error

* Equipment error or failure

* Act of God

* Deliberate silence for remembrance.

DJ-Disc Jockey : A radio presenter who links records.

DOG : Digitally Originated Graphic

A station logo or slogan permanently displayed on screen during a programme. Controversial due to "screenburn" issues.

Dolby Digital : Also Dolby D.

The standard for 5.1 channel (surround sound) audio. Six

discrete channels are used (Left, Center, Right, Left Rear Surround, Right Rear Surround, and Subwoofer).

Double pumping : Putting out two episodes of a show back-to-back, either to boost ratings in a given slot or to burn off episodes of a cancelled show.

Drive time : Drive time refers to the period of time where the majority of radio listeners travel to work. This is traditionally 6-10am and 2-6pm and is normally accompanied by the stations highest listenership. Commercials are normally more expensive during such times.

Drops : These are excerpts of TV, movies and other audio programmes that are used to accentuate programming.

Drop song : Temporary unselecting a playlist song to better accommodate an accurate clock hour.

DTH : Direct To Home

Television and radio programmes distributed by satellite for reception via a dish at the receiver's property.

DVB : Digital Video Broadcasting

The MPEG-2 based standard of digital transmission and

reception. Comes in variants according to the type of broadcast, eg DVB-T for terrestrial.

Encryption : The scrambling of a signal to allow reception via a decoder only be specific viewers, eg after the payment of a fee.

Feedback : The noise produced when the amplified sound from an output (eg loudspeaker) is picked up by the input (e.g. microphone) feeding that speaker.

FCC : Federal Communications Commission

The regulator of broadcasting in the United States.

Format Clock : A format clock is a diagram produced by a programme director or a producer to illustrate where each programming element appears in a typical hour.

FPS : Frames per second

The number of times the television is refreshed in a second of time. As a rule of thumb, this is the same as the local Alternating Current electricity supply - 60 Hz or 50 Hz.

Front Cell : The act of introducing a song about to be played.

Gain : Volume

GHz : Gigahertz

Thousand million cycles per second. The measurement for satellite frequencies.

Hammocking : Placing a new or poorly-performing programme between two established popular programmes in order to boost viewing figures.

HDTV : High Definition Television

In modern terms, broadcasting using a line standard of greater than 1000. Prior to World War II, "high definition" was used to mean a line standard greater than 240 lines.

Hit The Post : Where a DJ continues to talk right up to the point where the vocals commence.

Ident : A station's symbol or logo, often accompanied by music, a jingle or an animation.

ITU : International Telecommunications Union

Originally the International Telegraph Union, the ITU is the international organization established in 1865 to standardize and regulate international radio and telecommunications.

ITV : Interactive television

Systems that allow viewers to interact (e.g. play games, shop for related items or find further information) either two-way, via a telephone line, or one-way, via MHEG graphics.

ITV : Independent Television

The UK's first commercial television network.

Jingle : A produced programming element usually in the form of vocals to accompanying music often produced in-house to identify the show, DJ or the station.

kHz : Kilohertz

Thousand cycles per second. kHz is used to measure mediumwave and often shortwave frequencies.

Letterbox : The appearance of black bars at the top and bottom of a picture when 16:9 or 14:9 widescreen material is shown on 4:3 sets. See also pillar box and postage stamp.

Liner : A piece of written text that the DJ says over the intro of a song or between spots and songs. Liners are designed to invoke the imagination.

Line standard : The number of lines broadcast to make up a television picture.

Generally, 525 in NTSC areas and 625 elsewhere.

Live : Any programming which is broadcast immediately as it is being delivered (a live report); performed (a live concert or show); or captured (live news or sports coverage). Requires an unbroken communications chain without any intervening recording or storage technology. Considered the most exciting form of broadcasting, delivered "as it happens".

Live-on-tape : A pre-recorded program produced in real time, usually with a studio audience, for later broadcast. Requires precisely timed pauses for insertion of station breaks and commercials at time of broadcast. Typically employed for network broadcast across multiple time zones. Also applies to live broadcasting which is simultaneously recorded for rebroadcast at a later time or date.

Log : A written record of broadcasting. There are typically three logs:

* A Music Log recording what songs where played.

* An Engineer's Log detailing technical production settings.

* A Commercial Log recording which commercials were played during the day.

See also PASB.

Macrovision : A trademarked system designed to prevent unauthorised copying of video material.

MHz : Million cycles per second.

The bandwidth area for FM broadcasts and television.

Miscue : A mistake by the DJ or production engineer resulting in two audio elements being played at the same time, eg an interview and the next song.

NBC : National Broadcasting Company

A television network in the United States. Formerly also a radio network.

Network : A system which distributes programming to multiple stations simultaneously, or slightly delayed, for the purpose of extending total broadcast coverage beyond the limits of a single radio or television signal.

Nielsen Ratings : Survey of US viewers by the AC Nielsen Company to establish the audiences for individual programmes and their demographics.

NTSC : National Television Standards Committee

An American committiee formed to set the line standard and later color standard for broadcasting. Gave its name to the method of color reproduction used in the Americas (except Brazil) and in Japan.

Ofcom : Office of Communications

The regulator of broadcasting in the United Kingdom.

Optical : Generically, any on-screen graphic. Specifically, a graphic inserted between a programme and an advertisement or between individual advertisements.

OOV : Out Of Vision

A stage instruction noting that a character is not seen when speaking. Also, in continuity announcing, the practice of speaking over a caption rather than appearing on screen.

PASB : Programme As Broadcast

A BBC term for a (supposedly contemporaneous) log of a channel's output.

Pay-per-view : Reception of a scrambled film or sporting event after the payment of a one-off fee for that broadcast.

PIF : Public Information Film

A government-produced commercial, usually shown for free, giving safety information or advice.

Pillarbox : The appearance of blank bars on either side of the picture when 4:3 material is shown on a 16:9 widescreen television set.

Pilot : A one-off episode of a proposed series, usually in extended form, to gauge audience reaction. If successful, the rest of the series is made and the pilot becomes the first episode.

Pips : Slang term for the time signal broadcast by some radio stations at the top of the hour.

Playlist : The official songs that a radio station will play during a given week. The playlist is not usually chosen by the DJ.

Postage stamp : The appearance of a black border all around the picture, usually in error, when 4:3 material is converted to 16:9 and then back to 4:3 before broadcast.

Pot - Potentiometer : A round knob control for increasing or decreasing the volume on a channel.

Production element : A Production element is a piece of audio that is used in the final audio mix. This may include commercials, music, sound effects, audio effects (eg echo) station id or program signatures or announcements.

Producer : The person who performs or manages the day to day business operations of a station. Also the person responsible for an individual program - a radio producer or a television producer.

Promo : An announcement (either recorded or live) used to promote the station's image or other event.

PSA : Public Service Announcement

A commercial, usually shown for free, giving safety information or advice.

Quadraphonic : Sound reproduction utilising four speakers. Now superseded by Dolby 5.1 Surround Sound.

Ramp : An intro to a piece of music.

SB : Simultaneous Broadcasting

British term for the broadcast of the same programme from multiple transmitters.

Screenburn : Where a permanent mark is burnt into the mask of the TV screen due to prolonged display. Common with sets tuned to one channel for promotional purposes or on ordinary sets from DOGs inserted by broadcasters. Also known as Phosphor burn-in.

Sirius Satellite Radio. : American satellite radio platform.

Slipmat : A slipmat was a mat that was placed on a record deck between the deck and the record. Normally made by the DJ, it was cut significantly oversized when compared to a vinyl record. The DJ would cue the record to the beginning of a song and then holding onto the mat would turn the turntable on whilst the record stayed at the beginning of the song. The DK could then introduce the record and then release the mat onto the already spinning deck thus reducing the spin up speed to 33 or 45 rpm. The effect was to reduce the whirl effect produced by the turning on of the turntable.

Soundbite : A small portion (usually one or two sentences) of an audio recording (often an interview) used to illustrate a news story in the words of the interviewee (c.f. a quotation from a politician).

Sponsorship : In the United States, the practice of a company funding the making of a program in order to entertain an audience and sell a product. In the UK, an advertisement inserted between the end-of-part caption and the breakbumper.

Spot : A radio or television commercial.

Spot advertising : A commercial or commercials run in the middle of or between programmes, sold separately from the programme (as opposed to sponsors' messages).

Stop set : The place where commercials are played during a typical broadcast hour. There may be several scattered throughout a typical 60 minute period. Stop set length can vary much between local stations and even network programming.

Subtitles : Text version of a programme's dialogue, overlayed on the screen either at broadcast or at reception (often via Teletext or Closed Captioning) for the hearing impared or for when a speaker is unclear or speaking in a foreign language.

Sweeps : A period, usually in February, May, July and November, where the A C Neilson Company undertakes to record the ratings of all shows in all markets with all demographics. This allows networks and local stations to spot surprise hits and unexpected failures. It is also a time when a successful network will try pilot episodes of new shows, whilst a failing network will often put existing successful programs in place of poorly performing shows to boost average ratings.

Teaser : A part of a program played before the title sequence, usually featuring a cliffhanger or prefiguring the plot of the episode to follow.

Teletext : Electronic information inserted into the unused parts of a television signal and decodable by an equipped television set.

Television : The transmission of pictures and sound by radio frequency or cable for public reception.

Transponde : A physical part of a satellite that broadcasts the signal. In colloquial use, the satellite equivalent of the "channel" a television station is broadcast on (eg "broadcasting from Transponder 2C of the satellite").

UHF : Ultra High Frequency

Frequencies between 300 MHz (wavelength 1 meter) and 3.0 GHz (wavelength 10 centimetres), used for television broadcasting.

VBI : Vertical Blanking Interval

The blank area out of sight at the top and bottom of a television picture that allows the raster gun to reset. The space created is often used for Teletext and other services.

VHF : Very High Frequency

Frequencies from 30 MHz (wavelength 10 m) to 300 MHz (wavelength 1 m), used for radio and television broadcasting.

VJ : Video Jockey

A term invented by MTV as the television version of a Disc Jockey.

VTR : Video Tape Recorder

A method of recording television pictures by electromagnetic pulses on a sensitised plastic strip.

WARC : World Administrative Radio Conference

The regular meetings of the CCIR (now ITU-R) to allocate radio frequency spectrum.

XM Satellite Radio : An American satellite radio platform. Luminance in many color models used for television broadcast, such as YIQ and YUV.

Zoom : To go from a long shot to a clc se-up (or vice versa) with the camera. In the UK, the name given by Associated TeleVision to their idents.

NEWSPAPER VOCABULARY

5 W'S & H : The essentials of any story: who, what, when, where, why, and how.

Advertsing : Space in a publication sold to other businesses; display ads usually contain headlines, illustrations, copy, a call for action and information to identify the business

Alignment : Refers to the justification of text at its margins; left, right, centered, justified.

Beat : A specific area assigned to a reporter for regular coverage.

Bold : Type which appears darker than surrounding type of the same family; used for emphasis.

By-line : Indicates who wrote the story; often includes the writer's title.

Caption : The portion of the layout which explains what is happening in a photograph. Also called cutlines. Often includes a photo credit.

Column : A vertical division of layout which aids in giving structure to a page.

Dominant	:	The largest photograph on a layout.
Editor	:	Has overall responsibility for the publication.
Editorial	:	A type of story which serves to express an opinion and encourage the reader to take some action.
Ethics	:	A standard of conduct based on moral beliefs.
Fact	:	A statement that can be proven. Not an opinion.
Feature	:	A story written with some interpretation that goes beyond just reporting the facts.
Flag	:	The name of the paper that usually appears at the top of page one.
Graphics	:	The use of lines, screens, boxes, large initial letters etc. to enhance a design by breaking up areas.
Grid System	:	A system of layout in which the page is divided into small units which are filled in
Hammer	:	A form of headline consisting of a few very large words over a smaller subheadline
Headline	:	Large type designed to summarize a story and grab the reader's attention

Human Interest	:	An element of news that includes people or events with which the audience can identify; stories that are just interesting
Interview	:	A question and answer session between a reporter and source to get information for a story
Inverted Pyramid	:	A style of writing most commonly applied to news stories in which the most important facts appear early in the story and less important facts later in the story
Kicker	:	A short (one or two word) statement at the beginning of a caption that serves to grab the reader's attention
Lead	:	The beginning of the story which serves to summarize the story and/or grab the reader's attention
Libel	:	Written defamation; damaging false statements against another person or institution that are in writing or are spoken from a written script
News	:	Information delivered about an event shortly after it has occurred
Op-ed	:	Opinion/Editorial; refers to the pages in a publication that express the opinion of the writer
Opinion	:	A statement which cannot be proven.

Quotation : A statement make by another person included in a published story. A direct quotation is exactly what the person said and appears inside quotation marks. An indirect quote is a paraphrase of what a person said and does not appear in quotes.

Reporter : Person who researches and generally writes stories assigned by editors

Review : A form of editorial written to comment on a play, movie, piece of music or some other creative work

Sans Serif : Type with no extension at the letters which is easier to read at large sizes

Serif : An extension at the end of certain letters which make the type easier to read at text sizes

Slander : Spoken defamation; damaging false statements against another person or institution that are spoken

Spread : Two facing pages that are designed as one unit

Staff Box : A box containing the names of the staff members

Story : A block of text on a single topic beginning with some form of a lead followed by the body that

		contains quotations and transitions
Text Wrap	:	Adjusting the appearance of text to follow the shape of a graphic
Transition	:	The portion of the story which helps the reader move from one point to the next: helps a story flow, adds information, and explains other items in the story
Underline	:	A smaller headline set under the main headline that is approximately the same length as the main headline
White Space	:	The portion of a page with nothing on it used to draw a viewer into the other elements on the page

JOURNALISM GLOSSARY

Adobe InDesign	:	Desktop publishing program, now being used more widely in place of QuarkXPress.
Ad impression	:	Term used to describe the number of times an advert is seen. Advertisers usually sell space based on the exposure per thousand impressions (CPM).
ADSL	:	Asymmetric Digital Subscriber Line High bandwidth web connection.

Advance : A story outlining a future event. Also means to raise the priority of a story or an upfront payment for written work, particuarly long articles or text.

Advertorial : An advert in the form of a complementary editorial piece, usually labelled as an advert.

Analogue television : TV transmitted in radio waves as opposed to digital TV.

Angle : The approach or focus of a story.

Audit : An independent assessment of the validity of statistics used in adverts, newspapers etc.

AOP : Association of Online Publishers; industry body for UK web publishers.

Average issue readership : Number of people who have read the newspaper or magazine in the period that it was issued, also known as AIR.

BB2B : Business to business; describes a business whose primary customers are other businesses.

B2C : Business to customer; describes a business whose primary customers are individuals.

Background : Information given to a reporter to explain more about the situation and details of a story.

Back bench : Senior journalists on a newspaper.

Bandwidth : The amount of data that can be transferred through an internet connection.

Banner : Web advert, normally found at the top of a page. Typically around 468 by 60 pixels in size.

BARB : Broadcasting Audience Research Board, measures TV audience numbers.

BBC : British Broadcasting Corporation.

Beat : The area or subject that a reporter regularly covers.

Best boy : Broadcasting term for second-in-command of a lighting team.

Blawg : Weblog dealing with aspects of law.

Bliki : Combination of a blog and a wiki; a blog that can be edited by readers or an approved group of users.

Blind interview : An interview with an unnamed source.

Blog : An online commentary or diary often written by individuals about hobbies or areas of specialist interest. Also known as a weblog.

Blogger : A person who writes a blog.

Blogosphere/ Blogiverse/ Blogostan : All things relating to blogs and blog communities.

Blurb	:	Brief introduction to the writer, usually following the headline.
BRAD	:	British Rate and Data A company that logs every periodical that has to do with advertising in Britain.
Break	:	When a story is first published.
Broadband	:	High speed internet access.
Browser	:	A piece of software that allows users to view internet pages.
Bulks	:	Copies distributed free, normally for promotion.
Bump	:	To move the position or timing of a story.
Button	:	A small web advertisement, usually around 165 by 90 pixels in size.
Byline	:	A journalist's name at the beginning of a story.
Cable televisions	:	TV delivered into the home through an underground cable.
Campaign	:	The various stages of an advertising project from beginning to end.
Cap	:	Upper case.
Caption	:	Text used to describe a picture.
Cascading stylesheets (CSS)	:	Technique used for designing web pages. One file that defines the style for a whole site.

Chat rooms : An interactive part of a website where visitors can write messages to each other people in real time. Also known as forums and message boards.

Churnalism : Bad journalism; journalists that churn out rewrites of press releases.

Circulation : Number of copies sold by newspapers or magazines.

Clickthrough : When a reader clicks on an advert and is redirected to a new page. Advertisers sometimes buy adverts based on a rate per click.

Contempt of court : The criminal offence of ignoring court rules.

Convergence : Term used to describe multimedia newsrooms producing news for different publishing platforms.

Cookie : Small text file that is downloaded to your computer when you visit a site. The next time you visit, the site can use the file to remember details such as your login information.

Copy : Main text of a story.

Copy approval : A source or interviewer asking to see the text of an article prior to publication. (Always discouraged!)

Copywriting : Creating the text for an advertisement.

Coverline : Captions on a magazine cover.

Cover story : Leading story used on front cover.

Crosshead : A few words used to break up large amounts of text, normally taken from the main text. Typically used in interviews.

Cub : A trainee reporter. Also known as a rookie.

Cut : To remove text.

Cuttings : A journalist's collection of published print work. Also known as clips.

Cuttings job : Is when an article has been put together using someone else work, make sure credit is given to where it is due.

Cyber-journalist : A journalist that works on the internet.

Death-knock : Calling at the house of a bereaved relative or friend when reporting on the death.

Deck : Part of the headline which summarises the story. Also known as deck copy or bank.

Defamation : Information that is written by one person which damages another person reputation.

DHTML : Dynamic HTML.

Allows exciting things to happen when you move your mouse over words.

Digital television : TV transmitted in binary format, producing good picture quality.

Direct marketing : Sending advertising material directly to potential customers either by post, fax, email or information by telephone.

Dogblogging : When the upkeep of a weblog becomes a hassle.

Dowdification : Deliberate omission of a term or terms to change the meaning of a quote. Refers to journalist Maureen Dowd.

Downloaded : Copying a file from a website to your own computer.

Dropdowns : Name given to website menus that allow users to select from a list of options.

DPS : Double-page spread; can also be referred to as a spread.

Ee : Often used to indicate an electronic version of something, for example eNews, for an electronic newsletter, or eGovernment, to describe electronic government.

Editorialise : To write in an opinionated way.

Encryption : TV signals encoded so only paying subscribers can watch.

Endnote : Text written at the end of an article stating the authors credentials.

eSumers : Online or 'electronic' consumers.

eTail : Online or 'electronic' retail.

Exclusivity : When an advert appears exclusively on a page, rather than being in rotation with other ads.

Ezine : Specialized online magazines.

Feature : A longer, more in-depth article.

Fisk : Detailed word-by-word analysis and critique of an article. Refers to journalist Robert Fisk.

Flash : A program used to display design-heavy, animated content.

Flash : Short news story on a new event.

Flatplan : A page plan that shows where the articles and adverts are laid out.

Follow-up : An update on a previous story.

Font : Typeface.

Freelancer : Someone that works for themselves, usually on a contract-to-contract basis.

Freesheet : A publication that is free to consumers and generates its revenue from advertising.

Free-to-air : TV service recieved without having to decode or pay.

Freeview : Commercial free-to-air digital service, between BBC, BSkyB and the transmission firm Crown Castle.

FTP : File Transfer Protocol. A method of moving files usually used to transfer files from your computer to a web server.

FYI : For your information.

Get : A very good or exclusive interview.

GIF : A type of picture file, often used for images that include text.

Glossite : The website of a glossy women's magazine.

Graf : Paragraph.

Grip : A person that looks after the equipment required to make a TV camera move.

Hard copy : When the article is printed out on paper.

Hits : Number of downloads of every element of a web page, rather than the page as a whole. A page of 20 images, text boxes, logos and menus will count as 20 hits, so hits are therefore not regarded as a reliable measurement of web traffic.

Headline : The main title of the article.

Homepage : The front page of a website.

House style : A publication's guide to style, spelling and use of grammar, designed to help journalists write and present in a consistent way for their target audience.

HTML	:	Hyper Text Mark-up Language. Basic programming code used for the design and display of web pages.
Hyperlink	:	A link that redirects the user to another web page.
IImpressions	:	The number of times an advertising banner was viewed during a campaign.
An internet	:	Any network of connected computers.
The internet	:	The international network of interconnected computers. The World Wide Web, email, FTP and usenet are all part of the Internet.
Intranet	:	A private computer network inside a company or organisation for internal use only.Intro - Very important first paragraph, known as a 'lead' in the US.
Inventory	:	The number of advertisement spaces for sale on a web site at a given time.
Island position	:	An advert surrounded by editorial content in the middle of the page.
ITV network	:	15 regional franchises that make up ITV1. ITV is the Broadcaster that was formed by the merger of Carlton and Granada.

Javascript : A scripting language commonly used to add functionality to web sites beyond that which is achievable in HTML.

JPEG : Joint Photographic Expert Group. Common type of picture file used on the web.

Journalist : Someone who writes, researches and reports news, or works on the production of a publication.

Journo : Abbreviation for journalist or journalism.

Kerning : Adjustment of horizontal space between two written characters.

Kicker : The first sentence or first few words of a story's lead, set in a font size larger than the body text of the story.

Kill : To cancel or delete a story.

Kill fee : A reduced fee paid to a journalist for a story that isn't used.

Kittyblog : A pointless and boring weblog, possibly about the owner's cat.

LLayout : How the page is designed and formatted.

Layout sub-editor : A sub who specialises in laying out pages.

Leader : An article that shows the opinion of a newspaper.

Leading : Adjustment of vertical space between two lines.

Libel : A case for defamation. Defendent would need to show claims were true, fair comment or an accurate record of parliamentary or court.

Licence fee : BBC funding system.

Lobster shift : Working in the hours after a publication has gone to print. Also known as dog watch.

Mark : Correction.Mash up, mashup, or mash-up - a website or web application that seamlessly combines content from more than one source into an integrated experience.

Masthead : Main title section and name at the front of a publication.

Media Kit : Practical information available to potential advertisers regarding costs etc.

Microblogs : Blogs dealing with very specialised discussion.

Moblogging : Where individuals contribute to a blog using images or text sent from a mobile phone.

MPEG : Moving Pictures Experts Group. A file format used for digital video.

MPU : Known as a Messaging Plus Unit, a large square web advert usually in a central position below editorial. Typically around 350 by 250 pixels in size.

Multimedia	:	Term used to describe a range of different delivery formats such as video, audio, text and images, often presented simultaneously on the internet.
Multiplex	:	Single digital terrestrial TV transmission comprising of several channels.
Navigation	:	Structure that helps web users move around the website.
NCTJ	:	National Council for Training of Journalists, official UK accreditation board for journalism courses.
Netiquette	:	Online etiquette, *e.g.* reciprocal links.
News agency	:	Company that sells stories to newspapers or magazines.
Newspaper society	:	Industry body representing the regional press & local press.
NIB	:	News in brief—a quick summary of a story.
Nut graf	:	Paragraph containing the essential elements of a story.
NUJ	:	National Union of Journalists, a UK trade union.
Ofcom	:	Broadcasting industry regulator.
Off diary	:	An unscheduled or unpredicted story.
Off the record	:	Information that must not be disclosed.

On diary	:	Scheduled story.
On spec	:	Article that is written 'just in-case', but it will only be used if needed.
On the record	:	Information given by a source that can be used in an article.
Op-ed	:	A feature, usually by a prominent journalist, presenting an opinionated story.
Orphan	:	First line of a paragraph appearing on the last line of a column of text. Normally avoided.
PACT	:	Industry body representing independent cinema and tv producers.
Page Impressions	:	Number of times a web page has been viewed.
Pay-per-click	:	A common payment structure for web adverts; on an advert.
Pay-per-view	:	A single programme that the viewer has to pay for.
Pay TV	:	Paid subscription service for TV.
PDA	:	Personal Digital Assistant. A hand-held computer combining a phone, organiser and web client.
Phoblogging	:	Contributing photos to a blog.
Photoshop	:	Computer program used to edit photographs.

Pitch : Story idea sent to an editor by a reporter.

Pixel : An on-screen measurement. Most monitors display around 1024 pixels wide by 768 pixels high.

Plogger : Political web logger.

Podcasting : MP3 audio recordings that automatically download to a user's computer as soon as they are published online.

Point size : Size of the type face.

Pop-under/pop-behind : A web advert that opens under the browser window.

Pop up : A web advert that pops up on screen.

Post : To add a comment to a blog.

Pork : Material held for later use, if needed.

PPA : Periodical Publishers Association. Industry body representing UK magazine publishers.

Portal : A busy site often used as a starting point online through services such as messaging, news and searches.

Proof : Copy of a laid-out page ready to be corrected.

Prosumer : Marketing term used to describe professional consumers.

Puff piece	:	A news story with editorialised, complimentary statements.
Pulldown	:	Web text that is activated by a down arrow on a web menu.
Pull-out quote	:	Selected quote from a story highlighted next to the main text. Often used in interviews.
QuarkXPress	:	Desktop publishing program.
Quote	:	Record of what a source or interviewee has said.
Radio spectrum	:	Total capacity of radio frequencies that can be received.
Rate card	:	A list of advertising rates provided by a publisher.
Redletter	:	Exclusive, breaking news coverage of a major news event, printed in red type.
Reporter	:	Someone who writes and researches news stories.
Retraction	:	A withdrawal of a previously-published story or fact.
Revision	:	A re-written or improved story, often with additional quotes or facts.
Rich media	:	Artwork formats such as Flash, Java and DHTML that allow interactive or multimedia content.
Roadblock	:	The sale of all the adverts on your home page to one advertiser.

RSS	:	This began life as Rich Site Summary in 1999, then mutated to Really/Real Simple Simple Syndication in 2002, then Real Simple Synchronisation in 2005.
Run	:	To publish a story.
Sacred cow	:	News or promotional material which a publisher or editor demands be published, often for personal reasons.
Serif and Sans serif	:	Plain font type with or without lines perpendicular to the ends of characters.
Satellite television	:	TV recieved through a satellite dish.
Scoop	:	An exclusive or first-published story.
Search box	:	A tool that allows users to enter a word or phrase to search a database.
Serif	:	Font type with horizontal lines on the ends of characters.
Server	:	A computer that hosts the pages of a web site.
Shockwave	:	Software that allows the user to play multimedia animations; published by Macromedia.
Skyscraper	:	A vertical banner advert, usually at one side of a web page and 60 × 468 pixels in size.
Source	:	An individual who provides information for a story.

Splash : Front page story.

Standfirst : Line of text after the headline that gives more information about the article.

Stet : Proofreader's mark for 'restore to condition before mark up'.

Standfirst : Brief one-line introduction to a story, usually following the headline.

Sticky content : Content that encourages users to stay on one site for as long as possible.

Strapline : Similar to a subhead or standfirst, but used more as a marketing term.

Streaming : Watching or listening to video or audio in real time, rather than downloading files.

Style guide : A publications in-house guide to use and style of grammar, spelling, capitalisation etc.

Sub-editor : The person that checksand edits a reporters' work and adds headlines and standfirsts.

Subhead : A smaller one-line headline for a story.

Superstitials : A type of rich media advert that downloads gradually without obscuring other content on the page; usually more popular than pop ups.

Tabloid - Smaller print newspaper size.

Technobabble - Confusing technical jargon.

Teeline - A form of shorthand.

Terrestrial television - TV sent through a beam transmitter directly into the home.

Testimonial - Endorsement of a product, often by a celebrity or well-respected client.

TK - Proofreader's insertion mark for data to come. Sometimes written as TKTK.

Tie in - Placing the facts of a new story within the context of past events. Also known as a tie back.

Tip - A lead of piece of new information about a new story.

Top heads - Headlines at the top of a column.

Traffic - Amount of users recorded by a website.

Unique users - The number of individual users, as identified by unique computer addresses, that visit a web site.

Upload - To publish a file on the internet.

URL - Uniform Resource Locator, technical name for a web address.

User - A visitor or reader on a web site.

User-genereated content - Material created and submitted to sites by its users - such as photos, video footage, comments, articles etc.

Warblogs - Opinionated and political web logs.

Webcasting - Online visual and/or audio broadcasts, usually in real time.

Webmercials - Similar format to television adverts used online.

Weminar - A seminar on the internet.

Widow - Last line of paragraph appearing on the first line of a column of text.

Wi-fi - Wireless internet or network connection.

Wiki - A information site that can be edited and added to by readers.

Wikipedia - an online Wiki encyclopedia.

Wires - Stories or photographs sent electrically to your desktop.

Wob - White text on a black or other coloured background.

A GLOSSARY OF IMPORTANT CONCEPTS

Advertisement: A public notice or announcement usually paid for, about things for sale.

Angle: To give a specific aspect, bias, or point of view to a story or report.

Article: A complete piece of writing on a single subject; it is nonfiction.

Attribute: To give someone the proper credit for what he or she has said or written.

Byline: A line between the headline and the article, telling who wrote the article.

Caption: The copy (what is written) underneath a photograph

Cartoon or Comic Strip: A drawing, as in a newspaper,

caricaturing or symbolizing, often satirically, some event, situation, or person of interest. Or a humorous drawing, often with a caption.

Column : An article that appears regularly. It is written by one writer or about a special subject.

Click to do activities : Editor's Opinion, and Opinion Columns

Communications : A giving or exchanging of information, signals, or messages by talk, gestures, writing, etc. Or a system for sending and receiving messages, as by telephone, radio, etc.

Editorial : A column written by the editor that expresses his or her opinion about a particular subject of interest.

Ethics in Journalism : The code of morals that journalists are supposed to uphold. These include a commitment to revealing the truth, objectively and without being influenced by self-interest, maintaining the secrecy of sources, and attributing what is said to the appropriate source.

Click to see : Did you Know? Learn About Research Techniques

Feature : A carefully researched article, that either explains, interprets and/or provides background or

		tells of interesting, unusual occurrences that interest the reader. Feature stories sometimes have emotional, personal, and/or humorous slants.
Click to do	:	Feature Article, and to see: Did you Know?--Writing Feature Articles
Headline	:	The title of the article or column.
Click to see activity	:	News Headlines
Interview	:	A meeting in which a person is asked about views, activities; as by a reporter on a radio or a published account.
Click to do activity	:	Interview
Investigative Reporting	:	Reporting that requires a careful search to uncover facts and determine the truth.
Click to do activity	:	Investigative Report
Journalism	:	The work of gathering, writing, editing, and publishing or disseminating news, as through newspapers and magazines or by radio and television.
Layout	:	The way the newspaper is designed and laid out on the page.
Mass Media	:	Those means of communication that reach and influence large numbers of people, especially newspapers, popular magazines, radio and television.

News article	:	It presents, as objectively as possible, the facts about the latest news events.
News brief (or News Item)	:	The basic structure for a newspaper article.
Click to see	:	Did You Know? Basic News Brief Structure or to do: News Item
Objectivity	:	The state or quality of being without bias or prejudice; detached, impersonal. The journalist's job is to report the facts, not colored by his personal opinion; except in the case of opinions or editorials.
Opinion	:	Letters or articles that express the subjective opinion of the writer.
Click to do activity	:	Opinion Columns
Photography	:	Each article must be accompanied by an appropriate photograph and caption. Photographs should be colorful, interesting, clear and well composed.
Click to do activity	:	Pictures Worth 1,000 Words
Plagiarism	:	The act of taking ideas and writings from another and passing them off as one's own.
Profile	:	A short biography of an interesting person. It is usually based on an interview with the person.

Click to do activity : Profile

Report : An article meant to tell a story and inform.

Click to do activity : News Item.

Review : An article that presents a critic's opinion about an artist's work (for example: books, plays, movies, television and dance).

Subjectivity : The state or quality of being effected by the feelings or temperament of the subject or person thinking. (It is extremely important for us to teach our students to distinguish between subjective and objective journalism. Even though it is presented in black and white that does not mean that it is free from the writer's opinion.)

Survey : It collects the demographic profile of the reader and their opinions about a subject that has been chosen for study.

Target Audience : Who are the readers of the newspaper? The editors and journalists must gear themselves towards writing what will interest this population, in order for the newspaper to be successful.

Yellow Journalism : The use of cheaply sensational or unscrupulous methods in newspapers to attract and influence the readers. (The New

York World of 1895 would print the "Yellow Kid" comic strip in yellow ink to attract readers.)

Click to do activity : Celebrity Watch.

Advertisement : The promotion of a product or service.

Advertising manager : The person who oversees the sales representatives who sell space to advertisers, and ensures that ads are in the appropriate section.

Advertorial : An advertisement section in a magazine that looks like an article or a feature.

Advocacy : A style of journalism in which a reporter takes sides in controversial issues and develops a point of view.

A style of journalism which is opposite of mainstream journalism, in which reporters are expected to be objective.

Angle : Particular emphasis of a media presentation, sometimes called a slant.

Attribution : Credit given to who said what or the source of facts.

B-roll : Video images shot specifically to be used over a reporter's words to illustrate the news event or story, to cover up audio edits of quotes (to avoid the jerking head effect), or to cover

		up bad shots (out of focus, poorly lighted, etc.)
Background	:	Information that is not intended for publication.
Bias	:	A position that is partial or slanted.
Broadcast feature	:	Longer than usual broadcast news story that gives reporters 5-25 minutes (compared to usual 30-60 seconds) to develop a deeper look at a news event, trend, or individual.
		The broadcast equivalent of a newspaper feature story; also known as "television magazine piece" or radio feature.
By-line	:	The name of the reporter.
Canadian press	:	National news agency set up by the daily newspapers of Canada to exchange news among themselves and with international news agencies.
Caption	:	Copy which accompanies a photograph or graphic.
Classified ads	:	Categories of products or services.
		Short, direct text ads which clearly indicate WHAT is being advertised, the PRICE, WHERE, and HOW the advertiser can be contacted.
Column	:	An article in which a writer or columnist gives an opinion on a topic.

Commercial : An advertisement that is presented on television, radio, or film.

Conflict of interest : The conflict that is created when a writer allows personal interests (friendship, family, business connections, etc.) to influence the outcome of the story.

Copy : The words of an article, news story, or book.

Any broadcast writing, including commercials.

Any written material intended for publication, including advertising.

Copyreader : The person who "proofreads" copy as it comes in, checking for spelling, punctuation, accuracy of style, and clarity.

Credibility : Believability of a writer or publication

Date line : The place the story was filed.

Deck : A smaller headline which comes between the headline and the story.

Display ads : Ads that include a visual image to advertise a product or service.

Editor : The person who "edits" a story by revising and polishing.

The person whose job is to approve copy when it comes in

		and to make decisions about what is published in a newspaper or magazine.
Editorial	:	An article expressing a newspaper or magazine owner's or editor's position on an issue.
Facts sheet	:	A page of significant information prepared by Public Relations people to help news media in covering a special event.
Feature article	:	The main article on the front page of a newspaper, or the cover story in a magazine.
Five Ws and H	:	The primary questions a news story answers --Who? What? When? Where? Why? How?
Gatekeepers	:	People who determine what will be printed, broadcast, produced, or consumed in the mass media.
Gobbledygook	:	Language that is unnecessarily complicated, unclear, wordy, or includes jargon.
Gutter	:	Narrow margin of white space in the center area in a magazine, newspaper, or book, where two pages meet.
Hard news stories	:	Factual accounts of important events, usually appearing first in a newspaper.
Headline	:	The "title" of a newspaper or magazine story.

Human interest story : A story that focuses on the human side of news and often appeals to the readers' emotion.

Inverted pyramid : The structure of a news story which places the important facts at the beginning and less important facts and details at the end, enabling the editor to cut bottom portion of the story if space is required.

Investigative journalism : A story that requires a great amount of research and hard work to come up with facts that might be hidden, buried, or obscured by people who have a vested interest in keeping those facts from being published.

Jargon : Any overly obscure, technical, or bureaucratic words that would not be used in everyday language.

Journalese : A type of jargon used by newspaper writers

Language used by journalists that would never be used in everyday speech.

Jump line : Line of type at the bottom of a column which directs the reader to somewhere else in the paper where the story is completed, allowing more space for stories to begin on the front page.

Kicker : An ending that finishes a story with a climax, surprise, or punch line.

Layout editor : The person who begins the layout plan, considering things like placement and amount of space allotted to news and advertising copy, graphics, photos, and symbols.

Lead : The first sentence or first few sentences of a story.

Libel : Publishing in print (or other media) false information that identifies and deframes an individual.

Managing editor : The person who co-ordinates all news departments by collecting all copy and ensuring that all instructions for printer or typist are clear and consistent.

The person who meets and consults with the staff to make a plan.

Masthead : The "banner" across the front page which identifies the newspaper and the date of publication.

The publication information on the editorial page.

Media relations : A function of public relations that involves dealing with the communications media in seeking publicity for, or responding to media interest in, an organization.

Morgue : Newsroom library.

News angle : The aspect, twist, or detail of a feature story that pegs it to a news event or gives it news value for the reader.

Newspaper styles : Styles of various newspapers including dailies, tabloids, and weeklies

Newsspeak : Language that distorts, confuses, or hides reality.

Off the record : Something a source does not want repeated in a news story.

Op-ed page : a page in a newspaper that is opposite the editorial page, and contains columns, articles, letters for readers, and other items expressing opinions.

Package : A completed television news story on tape, which is edited before a news show goes on air and contains reporter's stand-ups, narration over images, and an out-cue for the anchor to start speaking at the end of the tape.

Paraphrase : An indirect quote or summary of the words the news maker said.

Photos : Still images which communicate the photojournalist's angle or perceived reality.

Pix : Short for pictures.

Plagiarism : Using the work of another person (both written words and intellectual property) and calling that work your own.

Public affairs : Various activities and communications that organizations undertake to monitor, evaluate, influence, and adjust to the attitudes, opinions, and behaviours of groups or individuals who constitute their publics

Reporters : The people who gather facts for the stories they are assigned to write.

Rules : Lines used to separate one story from another on a newspaper page.

Screens : Shaded areas of copy in a newspaper.

Sidebar : A column of copy and/or graphics which appears on the page of a magazine or newspaper to communicate information about the story or contents of the paper.

Slander : Similar to libel, but spoken instead of published.

Soft news : Stories that are interesting but less important than hard news, focusing on people as well as facts and information and including interviews, reviews, articles, and editorials.

Sound bite : The videotaped quote in television news.

Source : A person who talks to a reporter on the record, for attribution in a news story

Spin : Hidden slant of a press source, which usually casts the client in a positive light.

Stand-up : A reporter's appearance in a TV news story.

Usually a head and shoulders shot which features the reporter talking into a microphone at the scene of the news event, often used as a transition, or at the beginning or ending.

Style : Conformity of language use by all writers in a publication (e.g., AP style is conformity to the rules of language according to the Associated Press).

Summary lead : The traditional journalism tool used to start off most hard news stories.

The first few sentences of a news story which usually summarizes the event and answers the questions: Who? What? When? Where? Why? How?

Super : A video effect that allows the television station to print and superimpose the name of a news source over his or her image when the source is shown talking in a news story.

Tabloid : Technically, a publication half the size of a standard newspaper page; but commonly, any newspaper that is splashy and heavily illustrated.

		A "supermarket" tabloid that stresses dramatic stories, often about sensational subjects.
Target audience	:	A specific group of people that media producers or advertisers want to reach.
Transition	:	A rhetorical device used in writing to move the story smoothly from one set of ideas to the next by finding a way to connect the ideas logically.
Trend story	:	A feature story that focuses on the current fads, directions, tendencies, and inclinations of society.
Video press release	:	A press release for television, prepared on tape, complete with images and sound which can be used by the news media without additional permission or editing.
Voice	:	A writer's development of distinctive characteristics and idiosyncrasies of language use that make his or her writing as easily recognizable as the inflections, tone, and pronunciation of speech that make a person's vocalized speech pat terns distinctive.
Wire services	:	Services that provide news from around the world to publications that subscribe for a fee (e.g., Associated Press, Canadian Press, Reuters, and United Press International).

Co-operatives that share news stories among members (e.g., Canadian Press).

World Wide Web : Large directory of information on the Internet.

GLOSSARY OF JOURNALISM TERMS

Assignment : A particular job given to reporters by editors. Sometimes reporters suggest their own assignments, but they must get an editor's approval before beginning work.

Dateline : The place-names at the beginning of a story that tell the reader where the story occurred. A dateline includes the name of a city or town, and sometimes the country. Before high-speed transmission of data, it also included the date, which is why it is called a "dateline."

Deadline : A time given to a reporter by which he/she must turn in a story.

Editor : A journalist who works closely with reporters, giving out assignments and deadlines and helping them craft their stories.

Journalist : Someone who works in the news gathering business, such as a photographer, editor or reporter.

Newsroom : An office where journalists work.

Photographer : A journalist who takes photos.

Pulitzer Prize : Pulitzer Prizes are annual awards for achievements in American journalism, letters, drama and music. The prizes have been awarded by Columbia University in New York City since 1917, on the recommendation of a Pulitzer Prize Board. Fourteen prizes are given in journalism. The award is named after Joseph Pulitzer, American newspaper publisher, who endowed the journalism school and the awards.

Reporter : A journalist who gathers information and writes news stories.

Scoop : An advantage gained over competitors by publishing a news item first. Often, a news item itself is a called a scoop when no one else has that news item.

Included are specialized terms concerning the two areas most involved in publishing as school newspaper.

For convenience, they are divided into two sections: desktop publishing and journalism. Since some apply to both, check the second if not found in the first.

JOURNALISM TERMS

Ad	:	Abbreviation for advertisement.
Advance (advance story)	:	news of an event to occur in the future.
All caps	:	A word or word written in all capital letters.
AP	:	Abbreviations for Associated Press, a news-gathering service.
Banner	:	Type of headline stretching full width, usually at the top of a page; also called a streamer.
Beat	:	News source that a reporter is assigned to cover regularly.
Box	:	Material enclosed, either completely or partially, by a printed rule.
Byline	:	The name and identification of a story's author.
Caption	:	The heading placed above a photograph; sometimes used to refer to the descriptive copy below a photo.
Center of visual interest (CVI)	:	The dominate item on a page - usually a photo, graphic or headline.
Classified advertising	:	Ads run in small type in a separate section, which is often classed into different categories, such as "Help wanted" or "Lost and found".

Column (1) : A type of feature that is regularly run in a paper, featuring a single writer.

Column (2) : The vertical sections of type, which may have varying widths to story on a page.

Column width : The actual measurement in picas or inches; also measured in character count as a way to determine the character count of the entire story.

Copy : A story or article written for a newspaper; also used to describe a page or block to text.

Copyreading : Checking copy for errors before it is entered into computer or receives its final rewrite.

Crop : To eliminate unwanted portions of a photo to emphasize its center of interest.

Cut : Term for a newspaper photo or art, taken from engraving parlance.

Cutoff test : Reporter's check that final-paragraphs are not essential to story.

Cutline : The descriptive copy below a photo.

Dateline : Line at beginning of news story giving point of origin, if not local, and date, if significant.

Deadline	:	Time at which job must be handed in or completed to make issue date of publication.
Deck	:	Each part of a headline in a single font, whether one or more lines (once used to define a single line of a headline).
Direct quote	:	The reproduction of a speaker's exact words, set within quotation marks and correctly attributed.
Downstyle	:	The use of a minimum number of capital letters in headlines and body copy, where good usage permits an option.
Editorial	:	An article that represents the paper's opinion
Editorial column	:	An article representing the opinion of a individual writer.
Editorializing	:	Inserting the writer's opinion into a news story, which should be written objectively.
Euphemism	:	A milder word used instead of another word, possibly offensive—not an acceptable way to soften a quote from a news source.
Feature story	:	an article of special interest with a quality other than its timeliness as main attraction.
5 W's and an H	:	The Who, What, When, Where, Why and How—the key questions answered by a summary lead.

Folio line : The heading of inside pages, indicating section, school name, issue date and page number.

Follow-up : A news story written after an event has occurred.

Graph : Short for a paragraph (sometimes spelled graf).

Hammerhead : A large headline of only one or two words, followed by a longer and smaller head underneath—the reverse of a kicker.

Headline : Lines of display type printed above a newspaper story, calling attention to relative importance and attracting readers to the story's content.

Headline schedule : List of styles and sizes, often with counts, for use in a newspaper.

In-depth report : A story that goes beyond the surface to discover the news behind the news; also called an investigative report.

Indirect quote : Using a version of a speaker's words without quotation marks. Example: He said that he expected to reject the plan.

Infograph : A chart, diagram or graph presenting statistical information, such as survey results and enrollment figures, in easy-to-grasp form.

Inverted pyramid : A method of writing a story using a summary lead and facts in diminishing order of importance.

Kicker : Short, lead-in phrase above main head.

Label head : A headline without a verb; to be avoided.

Lead (leed) : the first paragraph of a story (see also, under Desktop publishing).

Libel : Untrue statement or material that damages a person's reputation.

Masthead : List of the paper's vital statistics, including school name and address, staff members and other pertinent data, such as editorial policy; usually found on editorial pages.

Menu : In newspaper terminology, a front-page box or boxes announcing a paper's inside contents, sometimes called teaser (see also, under Desktop publishing).

Nutgraph : Paragraph giving the key details of a news story—the 5 W's and H—when a variation on the summary lead in used.

Objectivity : An attempt to write a story without showing bias or injecting the writer's opinion.

Photo release : A permission form used by photographers for persons in

		photos not taken at news events, granting the right to print the photo.
Plagiarism	:	Unauthorized copying of another's work. Reproducing copyrighted material without permission— whether words or art—is a crime.
Profile	:	Feature story about a person; personality piece.
Pull quote	:	Quote from a story or news source that is "pulled out" and set as a graph in a distinctive format and type to attract readers to a story and add visual interest.
Retraction	:	A printed correction of an earlier error in the paper.
Slug	:	One or two words that specifically identify a story, typed in the upper left-hand corner of work to be edited or processed; also includes reporter's last name, plus date/ time from edit menu.
Stet	:	A term meaning "let it stand" - or disregard a change that was previously marked or indicated.
Style	:	Rules regarding punctuation, capitalization, abbreviation, etc.
Style book, style manual	:	Compilation of style rules for a newspaper.

Summary lead : A first paragraph that contains the essential 5 W's and H of a news story.

Teaser : A front-page box or boxes announcing a paper's inside contents, sometimes called a menu.

Trademark : The legal, registered name of a product or business. Be sure to use capital letters when using such trademarked names as Kleenex and Coke, which are sometimes used generically.

GLOSSARY OF NEWSPAPER TERMS

Banner : A large type headline running across a newspaper page.

Box : An item or story ruled off on all four sides, usually with a heavy border rule and often with the background tinted with the text in bold to highlight the story.

Broadsheet : A page size usually double that of a tabloid. Quality national newspapers are broadsheet in size.

By-Line : The name of the writer. It usually appears just under the headline.

Coloured dyes : Are used to make the paper the degree of white required—look closely and you can see that different whites are slightly green, blue, yellow or pink. The weight of newsprint is calculated in grammes per square metre, most of it weighing between 45 and 48.8 grammes per square metre. Its grammage makes a huge difference in the cost of publication with many pages. Substantial savings can be made on handling, storage and distribution as well as original paper costs by using a lighter weight and of course lighter weights require less raw materials.

Caption : The descriptive line or lines accompanying an illustration or photograph.

Copy : Traditionally the manuscript prepared for typesetting, but in the age of desk top publishing systems, the story or text on a wordprocessing screen ready for placing on the newspaper page.

Crosshead : See subhead.

Cut-off : The full column depth of a page, including the margins. Different newspaper printing presses use slightly different sizes, webs, or reels of paper.

Dateline : The line at the beginning of a news story that says where and when the story comes from **Deadline**— the time limit for preparing material for a certain edition.

Deck : A headline section, usually a line or a subsidiary headline.

Desktop Publishing (or DTP) : Use of personal computers (PCs) for low-cost typesetting and page make-up using any of the industry accepted proprietary, off-the-shelf 'shrink-wrapped' or bespoke software packages.

Ear or Ear Piece : The small advertising space beside the paper's titlepiece on the front page.

Edition : Each issue of the paper (mainly national and regional daily titles) are usually published in several editions - both to cover different areas and to update the news.

Extra : An edition of a newspaper published at a time other than the usual scheduled ones.

Fount : Pronounced 'font' - the complete set of type of one particular face and size, available from numerous type suppliers/ manufacturers on computer disks.

Gutter : The space between columns and facing pages.

Layout : Traditionally a 'dummy' plan of the page, a scheme or make-up sheet. More often today the format of a computer set and designed page.

Lead story : The main story in the paper, or on a page, or the opening paragraph of a news story **Leader**—the opinion column expressing the newspaper's view.

Literal : Any error in typesetting or word processing of text, usually in incorrect spelling.

Masthead : The presentation on the front page of the newspaper's title. Correct term is title piece. Also called a flag Point the standard unit of type size, 12 points to a pica, the basis of print measurement **Process Colour**—usually taken to mean full-colour reproduction achieved by colour separation on individual pieces of film.

Reverses : The typographical elements that reverse or vary the normal use of black lettering on paper, ie, white-on-black, black-on-tint, white-on-tint; often abbreviated to WOBs, BOTs, and WOTs.

ROP run-of-paper : A term used to describe display advertising placed throughout the paper, as opposed to classified ads which appear in categorised sections, usually in the middle or back of a newspaper.

Scoop : Also called an exclusive, a story obtained by a newspaper to the exclusion of its competitors Splash the main story leading the front page of the paper.

Stand First : A kind of typographical aperitif, a sentence or two presented in display fashion to introduce a news story or feature and perhaps its writer.

Strap : Subsidiary smaller headline placed over a main headline.

Streamer : The main heading on a page, running across several columns but less than the full width of a page. See also Banner Subhead (or Crosshead), a sub-heading within the text of a story or article, often used to break columns of type and make the page more attractive or easy on the eye. A crosshead is centred in the column, a subhead usually set left.

Tabloid : A page normally half the size of a broadsheet. Popular national newspapers are tabloid in size White generic term for space. The non-printing portion of a page.

Widow : A lonely word making up the last line of a paragraph, to be avoided when it would fall at the top of a second or subsequent leg or column of type.

ABC	:	Abbreviation for Audit Bureau of Circulation, an organization that compiles statistics on circulation.
Ad	:	Advertisement.
Advance	:	A preliminary story concerning a future event.
Advertising	:	Commercial messages that announce merchandise or services for sale. The messages are printed in newspaper space paid for by the advertiser.
Ad flow	:	Refers to the computer system that shuffles classified ads within their categories so that they fit best on a page.
Agate	:	Type 5 1/2 points in depth, the smallest ordinarily used in newspapers (72 points equasl one inch). Usually used for sports statistics.
Agate line	:	A measurement that is one column in width and 1/14 of an inch deep.
Angle	:	The approach or perspective from which a news fact or event is viewed, or the emphasis chosen for a story. See slant.
Associated Press (AP)	:	A cooperative, worldwide news gathering service.
ACNA	:	Atlantic Community Newspapers Association, a trade association whose members all

publish community (weekly) newspapers in Atlantic Canada.

Assignment : Any news-gathering task given to a reporter.

Backgrounder : (1) A meeting with the press in which a source gives information not for publication.

(2) Informative, factual story that relates the history or background of a current news event in order to aid audience understanding.

Balloon : A cartoon device, used in comic strips and occasionally in other ways, that shows the words of a person coming directly from his mouth into the "balloon."

Bank : (1) Lower portion of a headline.

(2) Computer file in which stories are kept before they are placed in their designated page form.

Banner : A headline stretching across the top of a page; also called a "streamer" or "banner line."

Beat : A reporter's regular assignment, such as town council beat, police beat.

Binding : Any further treatment of stock after printing; includes cutting, folding, trimming, gathering, stitching and gluing.

Bleed : An illustration filling one or more margins and running off the edge of the page or border; used frequently in magazines and advertisements.

Blind ad : A classified ad that does not reveal the identity of the advertiser; responses are generally sent to a P.O. box.

Blind interview : An interview story in which the interviewed person is not disclosed; e.g., a "highly placed official," a source close to the mayor," etc.

Blow up : (1) To play a story beyond its news value.

(2) To enlarge something (photo, art, copy, etc.)

Body type : Type used in stories, not in headlines; generally under 12-point size; opposite of display type.

Boil or "Boil down" : An expression for condensing news copy.

Bold or Boldface : Heavy or dark-faced type. This is boldface.

Border : Boxes or frames around pictures, stories and advertisements. Borders are computer generated and are available in many different styles.

Box : Refers to type that is framed in a border to give it prominence. The box is sometimes "filled" with a shaded area.

Break : (1) The point at which a story turns from one column to another or "jumps" to another page.

(2) The time when a story becomes available for publication. News is said to "break" when it happens.

Bumped heads : Similar headlines running side by side that create monotony and the tendency to read across.

Byline : The author's name carried at the top of a story.

Camera : A large camera shoots a picture of each page once it is completely finished. The negative of the picture is used to create a "plate" that is used on the press. This process has been largely replaced by computers which place the image directly on the "plate" making the negative obsolete.

Camera-ready : Refers to anything that is in its finished form - no further changes are needed before it is published in the paper.

Canned cop : Term applied to publicity material sent by press agents.

Caption : Headline or text accompanying a picture or illustration; also called a cutline.

CCAB : Canadian Circulation Audit Bureau, an organization that compiles statistics on circulation.

CCNA : Canadian Community Newspapers Association, a trade association whose members are all the regional newspaper associations in Canada representing community (weekly) newspapers.

Circulation : The total number of copies of a publication distributed to subscribers and vendors in one day.

City editor : The editor in charge of the collection, writing and editing of local news.

Classified advertising : Advertising arranged according to the product or service advertised, and usually restricted in size and format. The ads are "classified" into various categories such as help wanted, autos for sale, apartments for rent, etc.

Clean copy : Copy requiring few corrections.

Clean proof : A proof requiring few corrections.

Clip : Abbreviation for a clipping from a newspaper or from the files of the newspaper's library.

CNA : Canadian Newspaper Association, a trade association whose members publish daily newspapers in Canada.

Colour : "Colouring a story" implies introducing an element of bias or editorial point of view. "Giving a story colour" means brightening the story with human interest material.

Column : (1) Area on a news page usually 10 to 14 picas wide or 8 picas wide on a classified page.

(2) Article appearing regularly, written by a writer or "columnist".

Column inch : A unit of measurement one inch deep and one column wide.

Columnist : A writer using the same space daily, such as Ann Landers, in contrast to a reporter.

Compose : To type copy into a computer file.

Composition : The overall appearance of a newspaper page.

Community Newspaper : Refers to newspapers that publish local news, advertising and opinion, monthly, weekly or several times a week but less than every day.

Condensed type : Type with characters that are narrower than those of standard width, permitting more characters per line.

Copy : (1) All written material

(2) Reproducing materials using a photocopier.

Copy desk : The desk where copy is edited, headlined and placed on the page it will appear in the newspaper.

Copy editor or Copy reader : A person who corrects or edits copy written by reporters, checks stories for accuracy.

Copyediting or Copyreading : Correcting, improving and marking copy to be printed.

Copyright : Legal protection of an author's exclusive right to his or her work for a specified period of time.

Correspondent : A reporter assigned to cover work away from the home office in another community, province or country. A "string" correspondent is not a full-time employee of the newspaper, and is paid according to the quantity of copy accepted by the newspaper. See also stringer.

Cover : To get all the available news about an event.

Credit line or Photo credit : A photographer's byline. The name of the person or organization responsible for making or distributing a photograph, usually appearing small type under the reproduced picture.

Crop : To change the composition of a picture by cutting part of it out. A picture may be cropped to remove undesired background, to create more impact or to adjust the photograph to available space on the printed page.

Crusade : A newspaper campaign to bring about a desired reform or improvement.

Cub : A beginning reporter.

Cut : (1) A drawing or illustration usually copied off computer disk libraries.

(2) To reduce the length of a story.

Cutline : The copy (usually only a few lines) that accompanies and gives necessary information about a picture or "cut."

Daily : Refers to newspapers that print a new newspaper each day.

Deadline : The last moment to get copy in for an edition.

Deck : A "bank" or section of a headline.

Dingbat : Typographic decorative device, such as a star or heart.

Display Ad : Advertising matter other than in-column classified ads. They usually have a border.

Downstyle : Capitalizing only the first word and proper nouns in headlines.

Drop : (1) Short for "drop head," a headline accompanying a streamer and based on the same story.

(2) A story that was planned to run and then didn't.

Dummy : A diagram or layout of a newspaper page showing the position each story, picture, headline and advertisement is to have.

Ears : Space at the top of the front page on each side of the newspaper's name where ads, weather news, index to pages or announcement of special features appears.

Edition : A press run of a newspaper. A large city daily generally has more than one edition a day - for example, "City Edition," "Provincial Edition," "Early Edition," "Late Edition."

Editorial : (1) An article that expresses the opinion of the newspaper's editors and usually also reflects the opinion of the publisher or owner of the newspaper.

(2) The department of the newspaper where news is gathered, written, edited and readied for publication.

Eeditorial cartoon : Cartoon that expresses an opinion about a news personality, issue or event.

Editorialize : To express an opinion in a news story or a headline. Editorializing in the news columns is not considered good journalism.

Em : Unit of measuring column widths. An em (for the letter M) is a square of any given size of type, and is most frequently used as the unit in measuring "pica" (the width of an em in 12-point type).

En : Half of an em.

Exchanges : Copies of newspapers received by a paper when it exchanges subscriptions with other papers. Some large newspapers have an exchange editor to scan these papers.

Exclusive : A story printed by only one paper; a scoop.

Extended type : Type with characters that are wider or have more space between them than those of standard width; fewer characters can be used in a line.

Extra	:	An edition other than a regular one. Today it is published only when an event of transcending news importance warrants it.
Face	:	The style of type.
Feature	:	(1) Any story that has human interest value, even though it is not news in the strict sense.
		(2) To give prominence to a story or to emphasize a particular angle of a story.
File	:	To send news by wire; also used to designate one day's output by a press association.
Filler	:	Short informational stories or advertisements, usually timeless, used to fill small spaces where needed.
First-day story	:	A story published for the first time and dealing with something that has just happened, as distinguished from a "follow-up" story.
Five W's	:	Who? What? When? Where? Why? - The questions usually answered in the lead of a news story.
Flag	:	The printed title (i.e., name and logo) of a newspaper at the top of the front page.
Flash	:	The first brief bulletin from a press association with

information about an important news event.

Flush : Even with the column margin. Type set "flush" has no indentation for paragraphs.

Folio : Newspaper name; date and page number that appear at the top of each page.

Follow-up : Story giving later developments of an event already reported.

Font : A complete assortment of type of a given design, style and size.

Four-color process : A printing process that reproduces a full range of colors by overprinting red, yellow, blue and black (The true colors are magenta, yellow, cyan and black).

Fourth estate : Traditional term for "the press" which originated in the 18th-century English parliament.

Freedom of the press : In Canada, the freedom granted in Section 1f of the Bill of Rights; in the United States, the freedom granted in Article I of the Bill of Rights.

General assignment : A reporter who covers a variety of stories rather than a single "beat"

Ghost : A "ghost writer" is someone who writes stories for another's signature

Glossy : A shiny-finished photographic print, generally easier to use than "matte-finished" prints

Gutter : The space or margin between facing pages

Halftone : A special way of photographing a picture so that it appears to be composed of tiny dots.

Handout : A press release; prepared material given to news people in the hope that it will be printed without change or that it will be helpful in preparing news stories hard news; important news; straight news reporting without interpretation or background material.

Head/Header : Headline.

Headline : Display type placed over a story summarizing the story for the reader; commonly thought of as the largest line of type across top of newspaper calling attention to the most important story of that edition.

Hold : "Hold for release" instruction to hold a story until the editor releases it for publication.

Hook : The stylistic device used by a reporter to draw a reader into the story.

Hot : A label given to an important story.

Human interest : Emotional appeal in the news. A "human interest" story, as compared with a "straight news" story, bases its appeal more on the unusual than on consequence.

Imagesetter : A computer printer capable of printing out camera-ready newspaper pages (including scanned-in photographs and artwork) on paper or in negative form.

Index : Table of contents of the newspaper, usually found on Page 1.

Insert : A flyer or magazine that is inserted into the folded newspaper after it has been printed.

Inverted pyramid : The standard news story structure in which facts are arranged in descending order of importance.

Issue : All the copies which a newspaper publishes in one day.

Jump : (1)To continue a story from one page to another.

(2) The continued material.

Jumplines : The continuation instructions of a story that is jumped to another page.

Justify : Computers add spaces between words or individual letters of type so that lines of a column are flush left and flush right.

Kicker : Small headline, often in italics and usually underlined, above and slightly to the left of the main head.

Kill : To eliminate all or part of a story.

Layout : (1) A sketch or drawing that indicates the arrangement of pictures and copy on a printed page. Used synonymously with "dummy."

(2) A combination of stories, pictures, etc., about a single subject.

Lead (pronounced "led") : The space between lines of type. This space is often altered so that stories form perfect boxes.

Lead (pronounced "lead") : (1) The first few sentences or the first paragraph of a story.(2) A tip that may lead to a story.

Letter to the editor : A letter in which a reader expresses his or her views in the newspaper; usually printed on the editorial page or the page opposite the editorial page.

Libel : Publication of material that unjustly injures a person's reputation.

Library : A newspaper's collection of clippings, books, files, etc.

Lineage	:	The amount of advertising printed in a specific period.
Line cut	:	A drawing or artwork that is in black and white without shadows or shades of grey. The opposite of a "halftone".
Linotype	:	A computer printer that creates one line at a time.
Localize	:	To emphasize the local angle in an out-of-town story.
Logo	:	Short for "logotype" - The specific design and way a title or company name is written. Artwork often accompanies the title.
Lower case	:	Small letter, in contrast to capitals.
Make-over	:	Rearrangement of stories on a page to provide for new copy or to change the position of stories.
Mark up	:	To put composition or editing instructions on copy or layouts.
Masthead	:	Statement of ownership, place of publication, executive personnel and other information about the newspaper, generally placed on the editorial page.
Modem	:	A device that uses telephone lines to transmit data from one computer to another.
Monotype	:	A computer printer that creates one letter at a time.

More : The word placed at the bottom of a page of copy to indicate that the story doesn't end there—more is coming.

Lineage : The amount of advertising printed in a specific period.

Morgue : Where old newspapers, clippings, cuts and pictures are stored.

National advertising: Advertising of trademarked products that are generally sold throughout the nation.

Negative : An image that is opposite the way it will appear in the paper. Dark areas appear light and light areas appear dark.

News hole : The amount of space left for news after advertisements have been arranged on the page.

Newsprint : A grade of paper made from recycled paper and wood pulp, used primarily for printing newspapers.

News services : News-gathering agencies such as Canadian Press, Reuters, Associated Press or United Press International that distribute news to subscribing newspapers.

Obit or Obituary : A biography of a dead person. Sometimes "canned obits" are kept on file in the newspaper's library to be used at the time of a prominent person's death.

Offset press : A printing press in which the inked image is transferred from a plate to a rubber roller, which in turn puts the ink onto the paper.

Off the record : Information not for publication, or at least not attributed to the source if used as background.

Op-ed : Page of comment facing (opposite) the editorial page. Some newspapers use this page for letters to the editor, articles by columnists, etc.

Overline : The caption above a photograph.

Pad : To make a story longer by using more words than are necessary.

Page one : (1) The first page of the newspaper.

(2)Important, as in "page one news".

Paste up : Art and photos used to be manually "pasted up" on a page before the technology existed to scan them into the computer and "paste up" electronically.

Photoshop : A computer program for photographs. Photos are scanned into the computer where the image appears on the CRT. The image can then be cropped and the size altered to fit a desired space.

Pica : (1) 12-point type.

		(2) Unit of linear measurement equal to 1/6 of an inch (i.e., six picas = one inch.).
Pix		:Abbreviation for pictures.
Plagiarism	:	Literary theft - passing off as one's own work that of another person.
Plate	:	A plate contains the image of several pages, in multiples of 2, and is installed onto the press.
Play	:	The emphasis given a piece of news. A story may be "played down" or "played up."
Point	:	The unit of measurement in which type sizes are designated; approximately 1/72 of an inch.
Precede	:	Material to be printed ahead of copy already set.
Pre-date	:	An edition issued before its announced date of publication.
Press agent	:	A publicity or public relations person.
Offset press	:	A printing press in which the inked image is transferred from a plate to a rubber roller, which in turn puts the ink onto the paper.
Press conference	:	Meeting called to give information to the news media.
Press release	:	Specially prepared statement for the news media. See handout

Proof : "Proofreading" to look over items before they are printed and mark errors and changes for correction.

Proofreader : Person who reads pages and marks errors for correction.

Public relations : The art or science of developing understanding and goodwill between a person, firm or institution and the public.

Publisher : The chief executive and often the owner of a newspaper or other publishing firm.

Pull-out section : A section of consecutive pages printed inside the newspaper that when removed becomes a stand-alone section, often on a special event.

Put to bed : Printer's term meaning all the pages of an edition are completed and the presses are ready to roll.

Q and A : Copy in question and answer form, as in verbatim reports of court proceeding.

Quotes : Quotation marks. A quote is a portion of a story that consists of direct quotations.

Railroad : To rush copy through to the paper without careful editing.

Register : Correct placement of printing on the sheet. In colour printing, register means the correct placement of each plate to the colours are laid down properly, without running "off-register."

Release : (1) Common term for a press release or publicity handout.

(2) To permit publication of a story at a specified time.

(3)In photography, a form signed by the person photographed to authorize use of the picture.

Replate : Also "makeover" to make a new plate for a page in order to correct a major error or to insert an urgent story received after deadline.

Repros : Reproduction proofs - not the actual page or artwork.

Reuter : The first news-gathering service, founded in Great Britain in 1849 and still in operation today.

Review : A writer's critical evaluation of an artistic event, such as a movie or play.

Rewrite : Literally, to write again.

ROP : (1) Run-of-paper news and advertising that appears in any part of the paper convenient to the make-up of the paper.

(2) ROP Colour - a term used in advertising, means colour printed on an ordinary newspaper press.

Rough : A preliminary layout not in finished form.

Run : (1) The territory assigned regularly to a reporter; a beat.

(2) A press run, an edition. A story is "run" when it is printed.

Run-around : Body of type to be set around an odd-shaped picture, as in a feature story or a magazine.

Running story : A story that develops over a period of several days or more and is reported from day to day or week to week.

Runover : Part of a story that continues on a second page.

Sacred cow : A person, subject or institution given special favor or treatment in a newspaper.

Schedule : A news editor's record of assignments.

Scoop : An exclusive story or photograph.

Sectional story : A major news story with different aspects, featured under two or more headlines.

Series : A group of related stories generally run on successive days or weeks.

Set : To type words into a computer file.

Shirt tail : A short, related story added at the end of a longer one.

Shoot : To take photographs.

Short : A minor, brief story.

Sidebar : A secondary news story that supports or amplifies a major story.

Skyline : A banner head that runs above the nameplate.

Slant : An angle of a story. A story is "slanted" when a certain aspect is played up for policy or other reasons.

Soft copy : Copy seen on a computer screen.

Source : A supplier of information. A person, document, etc.

Spot news : News obtained on the scene of an event, usually unexpectedly.

Spread : The display given to an important story; a double spread is one across facing pages.

Squib : A short news item; a filler.

Standing heads : Headlines that do not change and are usually kept in a library file on a computer so they are ready for instant use.

Stet : "Let it stand." Proofreader's notation instructing the printer to ignore a change marked on a proof; from the Latin "stetundum".

Story : The general term applied to any newspaper article written by a reporter.

Straight news :A plain account of news facts written in standard style and structure, without colouring or embellishments.

Stringer : A correspondent for a newspaper or a news agency, usually part time, who often covers a certain subject or geographic area. The person is usually paid according to the number or length of stories printed by the newspaper.

Style Book : A compilation of typographical and other rules formulated by a newspaper to make uniform its treatment of spelling, capitalization, abbreviations, punctuation, typography, etc. Most newspapers provide style books for their staff's use.

Subhead : Small, one-line headline inserted in the body of a story to break up the monotony of a solid column of small type.

Syndicate : An organization that buys and sells feature material of all kinds, such as comic strips, gossip columns, crossword puzzles, etc.

Tabloid : A newspaper of small page size, usually 11 inches wide and 16 to 18 inches deep.

Tearsheet : A full page of the paper, including the folio, that has been clipped out and sent to an advertiser as proof that his or her ad has appeared.

Text : The verbatim report of a speech or public statement.

Think piece : A background or opinion article.

Thumbnail : A half-column picture.

Tie-back : The part of the story that ties it back to something that has already been published. A tie-in is used to connect a story with some other, perhaps more important, story.

Tight : Generally, too full; applies to crowded lines of type, pages, sections, entire editions. A tight paper is one without much room for additional news or advertising.

Tip : Information that may lead to a story.

Tombstone : To place two or more headlines of similar size side by side. Eyes tend to read across from one head into the next.

Trim : To reduce the length of a story; same as boil.

Typo : Typographical error—a mechanical error in typing a story.

United Press International (UPI) : A worldwide news-gathering service.

Uppercase	:	Capital letters.
Up style	:	Editing style calling for extensive use of capital letters; opposite of downstyle.
Video display terminal	:	A computer screen.
VCC or VCP	:	Verified Circulation Controlled and Verified Circulation Paid, a Canadian organization that compiles statistics on circulation.
Want ads	:	Classified advertisements.
Widow	:	A single word or short line of type at the end of a paragraph, particularly at the top or bottom of a column or page.
Wire copy	:	Editorial matter supplied by outside sources, especially that transmitted by telegraph or teletype from news services.
Wire photo	:	The Associated Press service that transmits photographs, maps or other illustrations. The illustration is then reproduced electronically in the newsrooms of subscribing newspapers.
Wire service	:	A news collection and transmission service.
News services include—CP	:	Canadian Press news service.
CNT-CPT	:	Canadian National and Canadian Pacific Telegraph, for

		transmission of correspondents' stories
Reuters	:	World service based in the United Kingdom
AFP	:	Agence France-Presse—World service based in France
AP	:	Associated Press - world service based in the U.S.
TASS	:	Soviet Union news service
UPI	:	United Press International, world service based in the U.S.
Yellow journalism	:	Sensational journalism.

GLOSSARY OF NEWSPAPER TERMS

AD	:	Printed notice of something for sale (short for advertisement).
Art	:	Any photograph, map, graph or illustration.
Assignment	:	The event or situation a reporter is supposed to report on.
Bannera	:	headline running across the entire page.
Beat	:	The area of news regularly covered by a reporter (ie...the city hall beat or the education beat).
Body	:	The main part of a story.
Box	:	Border around a story or photo.
Break	:	Initial news coverage of an event.

Bullet : A large black dot used at the left edge of a column to mark each item in a series.

Byline : The reporter's name, which appears at the head of a news or photo story.

City Desk : The area of the newsroom where local news events are covered.

Clips : Articles having been cut out of the newspaper (short for clippings).

Columnist : A person who writes a regular column giving a personal opinion.

Copy : All material used for publication.

Copy Desk : Area of the newsroom where editing is done.

Copy Editor : The person who edits news stories and writes headlines.

Correspondent : An out-of-town reporter.

Cover : To get all the facts about a news event for a story.

Credit Line : The name of a photographer or artist below a piece of art.

Crop : To cut away unwanted parts of a photo.

Cut : To shorten a story.

Cutline : Explanatory information under a photo or piece of art. Also called a caption.

Dateline	:	Words at the beginning of a story giving the story's place of origin.
Deadline	:	Time at which all copy for an edition must be in.
Dummy	:	A diagram of a newspaper page used to show printers where stories, photos and ads are to be placed.
Ear Copy/Ear Lug	:	In either upper corner of the front page, on either side of the flag (sometimes used for weather, jokes or to call attention to a special feature inside); also called an ear lug.
Edit	:	To correct and prepare copy for publication.
Editor	:	A person who decides what stories will be covered, assigns reporters to stories, improves the stories reporters write and decide where stories will appear in the newspaper.
Editorial	:	An article expressing the opinion of the newspaper editor or management.
Extra	:	A special edition of the newspaper, printed between regular editions, containing news too important to hold for the next regular edition.
Feature	:	A news story that may not have late-breaking news value, but is timely and of interest to readers.

Filler : A story with little news value, used to fill space.

Flag : The newspaper's name as it appears at the top of the first page; also known as the logotype or nameplate..

Hard News : Urgent news, usually of a serious nature, found in the front pages of a newspaper.

Headline : Words in large type at the top of a story telling what the story is about; also called head.

Inverted Pyramid : Form for a news story where the important facts are listed first and additional details follow.

Kill : To take out or delete copy.

Lede : The first paragraph or two of a news story, telling who, what, where, when, why/how; also called a lead.

Market : People the newspaper wants to attract with its news and advertising.

Masthead : Detailed information printed in the newspaper stating names of the publication's publisher, editors and other top executives, usually printed in a box on the editorial page.

Morgue : A newspaper's library of stories, photos, biographies and other references.

Obit : Short for obituary, a death notice.

Op-ed : A page opposite the editorial page, where opinions by guest writers are presented.

Play : Emphasis given a story on a page.

Proof : Page on which newly set copy is reproduced so it can be checked for errors before being printed.

Release : Advance information about a story given to the newspaper by the source of the news.

Reporter : A person who finds out facts about a story and then writes the story for the newspaper.

Scoop : A story obtained before other newspapers receive the information.

Stringera : Part-time reporter, a correspondent.

Syndicate : Organization distributing columns or feature material, such as comics or advice columns, to many different newspapers.

NEWSPAPER GLOSSARY

Picture Dictionary

Above The Fold : The top half of the first page.

Ads : Paid notices promoting items available for sale or lease or candidates for office.

Article : A written piece about a topic.

Beat : The specialization of a reporter, for example, government, business, or sports.

Byline : The name of a reporter as credited near the top of a newspaper article.

Caption : An explanation of a picture or illustration, usually placed under the picture.

Classified ads : Advertisements placed by people and businesses to let people know about items for sale and available jobs.

Cropped : Shortened. Articles are oftened cropped by an editor so that they will fit onto the newspaper page.

Deadline : The time at which an article is due.

Editor : The person in charge of the content of the paper.

Editorials : Opinion articles, written by the publisher, editors, and columnists of the paper.

Feature article : Non-news general interest pieces, for example, an article on stamp collecting.

Five W's : Who, what, when, where, and why.

Freedom of the press : In the USA, the freedom of the press is guaranteed by the First Amendment to the US

		Constitution. In many countries around the world, there is no freedom of the press.
Headline	:	The title of an article; it is set in large, bold type.
Hook	:	Something written early in an article that grabs the reader's attention and makes the reader want to read the rest of the article.
Interview	:	A conversation with a person in order to obtain information. Reporters interview people to find out about the topic they are writing about.
Interviewee	:	The person who is being interviewed.
Interviewer	:	The person who is conducting the interview.
Inverted triangle	:	A diagram shaped like an upside-down triangle that notes the content of a newspaper article, listing the most important items first.
Lead (or lede)	:	The first paragraph of each newspaper article (the first paragraph); the lead should summarize the main facts of the article, telling the 5 W's (who, what, when, where, and why) and how..
Letters to the editor	:	Letters from readers—they appear in the letters to the

editor portion of the op-ed section of the newspaper.

News article : A piece that describes and explains a current news event.

Newspaper : A newspaper is a daily or weekly publication that contains news articles, editorials, and other items. Newspapers are printed on large sheets of inexpensive paper that are folded. Ads (and to a much lesser extent, subscriptions) pay the costs of operating a newspaper. Synonyms for newspaper are paper and rag (this is a disparaging term).

Nut graf : The paragraph that contains the core information about the story and tells the reader why the story is important.

Op-ed : The opinions/editorials section of a newspaper.

Publisher : The owner of a newspaper.

Quote : The exact words of your subject (the interviewee).

Rag : A disparaging slang term for a newspaper.

Reporter : A person who researches and writes an article for a newpaper.

Scoop : A news story that no other reporter has discovered yet!

Sidebar : A story that accompanies a main story, perhaps detailing a background event or a related topic.

Supporting paragraphs : Paragraphs following the lead; these paragraphs go into more detail about the topic, often including quotes and interesting facts. The less important information should appear later in the article, since the article may be cropped (shortened) by the editor.

GLOSSARY OF COMMON NEWSPAPER TERMS

Agate Line : A measurement that is one column in width and 1/14 of an inch deep. Used primarily for classified measurements.

Camera-Ready Copy: A pasteup ready to be photographed by the platemaker. Does not require any camera work, pasteup or type setup.

Color Separation : The operation of separating artwork into the four process colors by means of filters in a process camera or by electronic scanners. The result is four continuous-tone films (negative or positive), which when screened are used to make printing plates.

Column Inch : Area that is one column wide by one inch deep.

Cooperative Advertising : Advertising paid for by both the national (brand name) and the local advertiser. Also, advertising in which several normally competing firms get together to do a common selling job.

Cost Per Thousand (CPM) : Used in comparing or evaluating the cost efficiency of publications or broadcast schedules. For publications, it is determined by dividing the rate or specific advertisement cost by the circulation or number of readers. For broadcast media, it is determined by dividing the commercial rate of homes or people tuned in. In determining the CPM of homes and people reached, average audience is used. simply, the advertising cost to reach 1,000 units of audience.

Four-Color : Also called full or process color. Full range of colors obtained by printing magenta, yellow, cyan and black.

Frequency : The average number of times audience is exposed to a medium. Usually referred to as average frequency.

Layout : The design of an advertisement that puts visual elements into a pleasing and readable arrangement.

Linage : The total amount of space taken up by advertising, expressed in agate lines or column width times inches of depth. Can refer to a single ad, total ad space for a page, an entire paper or a total amount over some period of time.

Logo short for logo type : The name of the advertiser in art or type form that remains constant from ad to ad. Usually available in more than one size.

Pica : A typographic unit of measurement: 12 points = 1 pica or 1/16" (0.166"), and 6 picas = 1" (or 0.996"). Also, used to designate typewriter type 10 characters per inch (as opposed to elite typewriter type, which has 12 characters per inch).

Process color : Also called full color. Refers to the four-color process reproduction of the full range of colors by the use of four separate printing plates, one for each of the primary colors-magenta (process red), yellow, and cyan (process blue-and one for black).

Editing Glossary

Batch capture : The abiity of certain computer-based editing systems to automatically capture whole lists or "batches" of clips from source videotapes.

Capture card : A piece of computer hardware that captures digital video and audio to a hard drive, typically through a FireWire (IEEE 1394) port. A digitizer is a special kind of capture card which converts an analog video signal into a digital one before it captures it on the computer's hard drive.

Character generator: A device that electronically builds text which can be combined with a video signal. The text is created with a keyboard and program that has a selection of font and backgrounds.

Chromakey : Method of electronically inserting the image from one video source into the image of another through areas designated as its "key color." It is frequently used on news programs to display weather graphics behind talent.

Compositing : Superimposing multiple layers of video. Each layer may move independently.

Continuity : [1:visual] Logical succession of recorded or edited events, necessitating consistent placement of props, positioning of characters, and progression of time.

[2: directional] Consistency in camera-subject relationships in order to avoid confusing a viewer's perspective.

Crawl Text or graphics : Usually special announcements or credits—that move across screen horizontally, typically from bottom right to left. Produced with a character generator.

Cross-fade : Simultaneous fade-in of one audio source or lighting effect as another fades out; may overlap temporarily. Also called a dissolve.

Cutaway : Shot of other than principal action (but peripherally related), frequently used as transitional footage or to avoid a jump cut.

Digital video effects (DVE) : Electronic analog-to-digital picture modification yielding specialty image patterns and maneuvers: tumbling, strobing, page turning, mosaic, posterization, solarization, etc.

Digitization : The process of converting a continuous analog video or audio signal to digital data for the purpose of computer storage and manipulation.

Dissolve : Image transition effect of one picture gradually disappearing as another appears. Analogous to audio and lighting cross-fade. [See cross-fade.]

Dub : [1] Process or result of duplicating a videotape in its entirety.

[2] Editing technique whereby new audio or video replaces portion(s) of existing recording.

Edit decision list (EDL) : Handwritten or computer-generated compilation of all edits (marked by their time code in points and out points) to be executed in a video production.

Generation loss : Degradation in picture and sound quality resulting from an analog duplication of original master video recording. Copying a copy and all successive duplication compounds generation loss. Digital transfers are free of generation loss.

Hard disk : Common digital storage component in a computer. For video use, hard disks need to have: 1) an access time of less than 10 milliseconds; 2) a sustained throughput (data transfer rate) of 3 Megabytes per second; and 3) a maximum time for housekeeping of 33 milliseconds.

Jump cut : Unnatural, abrupt switch to/from shots identical in subject but slightly different in screen location. Awkward progression makes subject appear to jump from one screen location to another. It can be remedied with cutaway or shot from a different angle.

Montage : A sequence of shots assembled in juxtaposition to each other to communicate a particular idea or mood. The implied relationship between seemingly unrelated material communicates messages.

Nonsynchronous sound : Audio without precisely matching visuals. Usually recorded separately, includes wild sound, sound effects, or music incorporated in post-production. [See synchronous sound.]

Post production (post) : Any video production activity following initial recording. Typically involves editing, addition of background music, voiceover, sound effects, titles, and/or various electronic visual effects. Results in completed production.

Real time : Occurring immediately, without delay for rendering. If a transition occurs in real time, there is no waiting, the computer creates the effect or transition on-the-fly, showing it on demand.

Render : The processing a computer undertakes when creating an applied effect, transition or composite.

Rough cut : Raw, tentative edit of footage in the approximate sequence, length, and content of finished program. Gives preliminary indication of eventual actual work.

Safe title area : The area that will produce legible titles on most TV screens; 80% of the screen, measured from the center.

Synchronous sound : Audio recorded with images so the words sync with the mouth.

A/B : Roll

Assemble edit : Recording video and/or audio clips in sequence immediately following previous material; does not break control track. Consecutive edits form complete program. [See edit, insert edit.]

Compositing : Superimposing multiple layers of video. Each layer may move independently.

Continuity : [1:visual] Logical succession of recorded or edited events, necessitating consistent placement of props, use of wardrobe, positioning of characters, and progression of time.

[2:directional] Consistency in camera-subject relationships, to avoid confusing a viewer's perspective.

Cut : Instantaneous change from one shot to another.

Cutaway : A shot of something other than the principal action (but related), frequently used as transitional footage or to avoid a jump cut.

Digital video effects (DVE) : Electronic picture modification yielding specialty image patterns and maneuvers: tumbling, strobing, page turning, mosaic, posterization, solarization, etc.

Dissolve : Image transition effect where one picture gradually disappears as another appears. Analogous to audio and lighting cross-fades. Also known as a cross-fade.

Edit : Process or result of selectively recording video and/or audio on finished videotape. Typically involves reviewing raw footage and transferring desired segments from master tape(s) onto new tape in a predetermined sequence.

Edit decision list (EDL) : Handwritten or computer generated compilation of all post-production edits to be executed in a video work.

Editing : Uses two video sources played simultaneously, to be mixed or cut between.

Generation loss : Degradation in picture and sound quality resulting from duplication of original master video recording. Copying a copy and all successive duplication compounds generational loss.

Insert edit : Feature allowing a VCR to record a new video and/or audio segment in the middle of a program, without breaking the control track or disturbing what precedes and follows.

Jump cut : Unnatural, abrupt switch from and to shots identical in subject but slightly different in screen location. Awkward progression makes subject appear to jump from one screen location to another. Remedied with cutaway.

Linear editing : Analog, tape-based editing. Called linear because scenes are laid in a line along the tape. Has many disadvantages, such as the need to rewind and fast forward and the inability to insert footage without re-recording everything that follows.

Nonlinear editing (NLE) : Digital "cut and paste" editing that uses a hard drive instead of tape to store images. Random access allows easy arrangement of scenes in any order. Also eliminates the need for rewinding and allows for multiple dubs without generation loss.

Pre-roll : Slight backing-up function of camcorders and VCRs when preparing for tape recording; ensures smooth, uninterrupted transitions between scenes.

Rendering time : The time it takes an NLE computer to composite source elements and commands in it's edit decision list into a single video file so the sequence, including titles and transition effects, can be played in full motion (30 frames per second).

Time code : Synchronization system, like a clock recorded on your videotape, assigning a corresponding hours; minutes; seconds; frame-number designation to each frame. Expedites indexing and editing precision.

Time line editing : A nonlinear method of editing in which video and audio clips are represented on a screen by bars proportional to the length of the clip. These bars can be moved and resized along a grid whose horizontal length corresponds with the duration of the program.

Wipe : Transition from one shot to another wherein the new shot is revealed by a moving line or pattern. In simplest form, simulates a window shade being drawn.

FILM EDITING GLOSSARY

4-2-4 : The method of recording and playing back Dolby Stereo sound for film. The tracks are mixed down from their four-track format to a two-track form. It is this two-track version that is transferred to optical track and married with the picture. At the theaters, Dolby equipment expands the two tracks back into four.

Academy Leader : Leader which conforms to the standards set up by the Academy of Motion Picture Arts and Sciences. From the projection start mark on this leader, it is exactly eight seconds (12 feet in 35 mm, four feet and 32 frames in 16 mm) until the beginning of the picture.

Academy Roll-Off : A standard, established by the Academy of Motion Picture Arts and Sciences, for movie theater sound. It involves decreasing quite a bit of the high-frequency sound. This roll-off is what Dolby film sound tries to avoid.

Add-A-Plate : See Console.

ADR : Automatic Dialogue Replacement. See Looping.

Anamorphic : A method of getting wide-screen images from normal 35 mm film. In the shooting, a special lens is used which squeezes the image.

A matching lens reverses the process for projection. If you were to look at a frame of anamorphic film without "unsqueezing" it (such images would be called "squeezed") it would look like the image on a balloon after the air has been let out of it.

Answer Print : A timed (color-corrected) print of the film. It may or may not have a soundtrack married to it.

Assembly : A rough piecing-together of the cut, sometimes called a "rough cut." The assembly consists of all of the scenes shot, and usually runs quite a bit longer than the finished film.

B-negative : Takes which were shot and developed but not printed.

Balance Stripe : See Stripe.

Balancing : See Reel Balancing.

Base : The bottom side of the film. It is shiny, as opposed to the top part of the film -- the emulsion which is dull. Actually, the base is a plastic material onto which the three layers of color film stock (or the one layer of black and white) are glued. See also Emulsion.

Beep tone : A short tone which can be used to mark a specific location on a soundtrack. It is commonly used at the beginning of reels, two seconds before the beginning of the picture (nine feet after the start mark in 35 mm, three feet and 24 frames in 16 mm).

Bump : When two sounds are cut together it is possible that the background sounds will not match exactly. The effect of the different sounds cut together is called a bump. The tasks of "dialogue splitting" and "mixing" are designed to smooth out these bumps and end up with one seamless soundtrack.

Camera Original : The actual film that went through the camera on location.

Card : A particular kind of credit optical in which the names remain stationary, fading in and out.

Changeover Cue : The second changeover cue. When the projectionist sees it, s/he is supposed to switch the projection from one projector to the other.

Changeovers : The marks which are placed in the upper right hand corner of the frame to cue the projectionist to change from one reel to another.

Character Reel : A reel set up for an ADR session which contains one character's lines only.

Cheated Track : A piece of track which is cut into the work track purposely out of sync with the picture.

Cinetabs : Small tabs which are used for identification of individual rolls of film or sound. Also called "trim tabs."

Clapper : See Slate.

Click Track : A musical rhythm. Each click represent one musical beat. A click of 12/0 denotes that one beat of music comes every 12 frames.

Code Number : A number which is physically printed onto the edge of the film, in ink. It is used to identify pieces of film and track in the editing room and to keep the picture and track in sync. These numbers usually run one every foot. Also called an "edge number."

Color Cards : Standardized cards which contain a scale of colors. When these are shot, it is easy to tell just how far the filmed colors deviate from the actual colors. Such cards facilitate the color correcting of a film.

Color Correction : See Timing.

Conformation : A change made to a reel after it has been locked.

Console : A moviola with one picture head and two sound heads. Often a second sound head is attached onto a regular moviola. This attachment is called an "add-a-plate."

Core : A two- or three-inch diameter plastic disc which is exactly the width of the film. The film or mag is wound onto the cores for editing or projection. See also Split Reel.

Coverage : The various angles that a director shoots for a scene.

Crawl : A particular kind of credit optical in which the names move up or down the screen.

CRI : Color Reversal Intermediate. A particular kind of reversal (original) film which can be struck directly from another negative, without going through an intermediate positive stage, such as with an I.P.

CRI Print : A release print from a CRI, as opposed to an EK print.

Cut : The cut-together work picture and work track, either together or singly.

Cut Picture : See Work Picture.

Cutter Moviola : A type of upright moviola which has no arms on it, is easier to take film on and off of, and is gentler on the film than a regular moviola, all of which facilitates its use as a cutting machine.

Cutting copy : The work picture.

D-M-E Track : A M & E full coat track which also includes, usually on channel one, the mixed dialogue to be used as a reference for foreign dubbing.

Dailies : Every day during the shooting of a film, the director and some members of the cast and crew view the footage shot the preceding day to verify that everything is satisfactory. If it is not, some of the footage may have to be reshot. These screenings are called "dailies screenings" or "rushes."

Degaussing : The process of erasing all sound from a piece of magnetic stock or tape.

Dialogue Splitting : The process of separating work track pieces which bump together onto separate elements so that each may be treated separately at the mix.

Dissolve : An optical in which one image slowly changes into another.

Domestic Version : The major release of a film, in the United States and English speaking countries.

Double Reel : When the film is ready to be distributed, the 1000 foot editing reels are combined into 2000 foot reels for theaters. This is accomplished by combining reels one and two into Double Reel One, editing reels three and four into Double Reel Two, and so on.

Drop Shadow : A design for titles in which a small, darker, extra copy of the words is superimposed onto the title, slightly askew of it. This gives the words more readability.

Dub : See Mix.

Dubbing : (1) Mixing the film. (2) Looping.

Dupe : A copy. Picture is often duped onto a piece of black-and-white film. Such dupes are called "slop dupes" or "slop prints." When tracks are duped it is normal to ask for a one-to-one copy, to preserve the same volume level and equalization as the original track.

Edge Number : See Code Number.

Editing Bench : A wide table on which most of the editorial equipment sits. As a result, most of the physical cutting of the film is done on it. Both the rewinds and the synchronizer are on this table, as well as the splicers and a host of other equipment. Editors who edit their films on flatbeds do not use editing benches as much as editors who cut on an upright since the flatbed itself functions as the bench for most of their editing work. Sometimes referred to as the Editing Table.

Effect : (1) In picture, an optical or special photographic manipulation of the film.

(2) In sound, a specific sound, such as of a tire squeal or water dripping.

(3) Also used to mean a special manipulation of elements during the shooting of the film, such as the creation of rain or snow.

EK Print : A release print from the camera original, as opposed to an I.P. Print, or a CRI print.

Element : An individual sound track at a mix. Also called a "unit."

Emulsion : The top side of the film. It is dull, as opposed to the bottom part of the film -- the base -- which is shiny. Your lips will leave a mark on the emulsion side of film.

EPS : Electronic Post-Sync. See Looping.

Extension : In sound or in picture editing, a trim which is added to a piece already used in the film.

Eye Sync : The process of syncing up picture and track without slates. It involves finding points in the sound which can easily be located on the picture as well, such as door slams. Certain letters of the alphabet also provide good sync points, such as the letters b, d, k, p, or t.

Fades : Opticals in which an image gradually goes to black (fade-out) or emerges from black (fade-in). It is also possible to have images fade in from or out of other colors besides black, such as white.

Fill : Waste film. It is used to space out soundtracks within a reel to preserve synchronization with the picture. It is also called "slug" or "spacing."

Flash Frames : As the camera is slowing down at the end of a take it lets more light in. This shows up as a frame or two on the film where the image is very bright. Flash frames are handy for identifying the ends of takes.

Flatbed : A kind of editing machine. The separate film and soundtrack are run horizontally across this table-like device in sync with each other.

Flipped Track : Track which has been turned upside down, so that it will not read. Track is flipped so that it will be in sync and ready to be used in case it is desired by simply unflipping the track.

Flop Track : Track which has been turned around so that what was the left side of the frame becomes the right and vice versa.

Foleys : Effects, usually body movement of some sort, such as footsteps or clothes rustle. which is recorded in sync with picture.

Four-Stripe : See Full Coat.

Four-Track : See Full Coat.

Frame : An individual picture on the film. Each frame is exposed for 1/48th of a second. The camera shutter is then closed for 1/48th of a second while the film is pulled down to the next film frame, which is then exposed for 1/48th of a second. It is the rapid projection of succeeding frames, in which the position of the elements in the picture changes slightly from frame to frame, which gives the audience the illusion of motion.

Frame Line : The space between two succeeding frames.

Full Coat : 35mm track which is completely covered with oxide. As many as six tracks of sound can be recorded onto it. Other configurations are four and three tracks. For that reason, full coat is also known as "three-track," "three-stripe, "four-track," or "four-stripe."

Gray Scale : A standardized card which works exactly like a color card except that it shows gradated black-to-white rather than colors.

Handle : An extra few frames attached to the head and tail of an optical, beyond what is needed.

Head Trim : See Trim.

Hi-Con : A black and white optical stock often used for credits or special effects.

Hole : A portion of a soundtrack which has no sound in it.

IP/IN : The process of making a new negative of a film by striking an interpositive and then, from that, a new negative -- the internegative. In recent years, this two-step process was replaced by the CRI process. But advances in the IP/IN stocks now make this a preferable method for release printing.

I.P. Print : A release print from an I.P., as opposed to an EK print.

Interpositive : A positive film stock, used for optical negatives, sometimes called an "I.P." Technically, a color fine-grain positive print used for making color dupe negatives.

KEM : A brand name for a common flatbed editing machine.

Key Number : A number which is imprinted into the edge of the film negative. This number is then exposed on to the print film, giving a permanent record of every piece of film used in the movie. Also called a "latent edge number."

Latent Edge No. : See Key Number.

Leader : White-coated film which is used at the heads and tails of film and soundtrack. It serves several purposes. It protects the film itself since it is wound on the outside of the reels rather than the valuable picture. It also provides the thread-up necessary for projection. Since it can be easily written on, it is also used as identification.

LFOA : Last Frame of Action. The last frame on a reel of film or track before the leader begins.

Lift : Piece of cut picture or track which is removed from the film and stored intact, rather than being broken apart and stored as trims.

Lock : That point in the editing of the film when the picture editing is over. The cut is then "locked."

Loop : A piece of track which has been joined at its ends to form a continuous band. When played, it will go around in a circle until stopped providing a nice continuous sound.

Looping : Dialogue replacement. Sometimes called dubbing. Also called "ADR" or "EPS."

M & E Track : A mixed full-coat which has the music on one channel (usually channel two), the mixed effects on another usually channel three) and no dialogue.

Mag : Soundtrack stock.

Married Print : At no time during the shooting or editing of a film are the sound and picture on the same piece of film. It is not until the film is ready to go into the theaters that the two are combined, or "married," together. See also Optical Track.

Matte Shot : An optical in which part of one shot is combined with part of another to create another shot which did not exist to begin with. An example would be taking a shot of an astronaut shot in a studio, combining it with a shot of a scene which appears to be on the moon.

Mix : The combination of many sound elements -- dialogue, music, and sound effects into one cohesive and balanced soundtrack. Also called a "dub."

Mixed Mag : A single mono stripe of the final mix of a film.

MOS : Literally "mit-out-sound." Used to denote a picture take for which no sound was shot.

Motor Cue : The first changeover cue. When the projectionist sees it s/he is supposed to start up the motor on the other projector.

Moviola : A brand name for a common editing machine. The separate film and soundtrack are run vertically from the feeding reels onto the take-up reels in sync with each other. Also called an "upright moviola" to differentiate it from a Moviola Flatbed.

Moviola Flatbed : A brand name for a common flatbed editing machine.

Negative : Original film exposed in the camera.

Numbering Machine: A machine which inks code numbers onto the edge of the film and track.

One-to-One Copy : A sound transfer which is at exactly the same level and equalization as the original sound.

Optical	:	A piece of film which has been manipulated in some special way, after it has already been shot, to create some special effect.
Optical Track	:	The soundtrack on a married print. It appears as a set of squiggly lines at the left side of the picture. When light is projected through the optical track it is read by a photocell behind the film. This photocell decodes the patterns of the light into sounds -- providing us with the dialogue, music, and sound effects that we hear on a film's soundtrack.
Out	:	A take, no part of which has been used in the cut work picture.
Phasing	:	The hollow sound that occurs when two identical tracks are run in near-perfect sync.
Pick-Up-Shot	:	After a shot has been made on the set, the director sometimes wishes to re-do only part of the set-up. This re-do is called a pick-up shot since only part of the shot is picked up. It is slated with the same set-up letter, and the letters "p.u." are added at the end. For instance, a pick-up to shot 11A would 11Apu.
Pre-Mix	:	When many units are involved in a mix it is difficult, if not

impossible, to play them all at one time. In this case, several of them are mixed together and this new mix (called the pre-mix) will replace those many elements at the mix. Also called pre-dub.

Protection I.P. : See Registration I.P.

Reel Balancing : The act of apportioning the footage between all of the reels so that no reel has too little or too much film, and so that changeovers can be made without the audience noticing.

Registration I. P. : A certain type of interpositive which is printed in so particular a manner that the I.P. can be used as a replacement negative. For this reason, a registration I.P. is made whenever the original negative is being removed from the lab, so as to have a protection in case something were to happen to the original negative. A registration I.P. is, therefore, sometimes called a "protection I.P."

Release Print : The married print which is sent to theaters for showing. Normally, it is not made directly from the original camera negative, but is made from a dupe negative.

Rough Mix : See Scratch Mix.

Run-Out : The extra thirty feet or so placed at the end of any reel or unit going into the mix. This will prevent the mixer from running past the end of a reel when it is not desired.

Rushes : See Dailies.

Scratch Mix : A temporary mix used primarily to combine dialogue and music or an important sound effect. No attempt is made to correct sound problems. Also called a "slop mix" or "rough mix" or "dub."

Set : The location where the film is being shot.

Set-Up : (1) An individual camera position. A given scene will usually be covered with several different camera angles and lens sizes. Each of these is a different set-up. In American notation, each set-up for a given scene (say, scene 11) will be given a different set-up letter (11, for the master, and 11A, 11B, 11C, etc., for other angles).

(2) Can also refer to the editing room table equipment -- synchronizer, rewinds, splicing block, et al.

Single Card : A credit in which only one name appears on a card.

Slate : The black-and-white board which is struck together at the beginning of every take. It is used to provide a visible and audible sync point as well as providing a visual record of the set-up and take numbers of the take. Also called a "clapper."

Slop Dupe : See Dupe.

Slop Mix : See Scratch Mix.

Slop Print : See Dupe.

Slug : See Fill.

SMPTE Code : A method of sync which is used for tape media, such as music recording tape or videotape.

Sound Reader : An amplifier. Sound from the track is picked up from the sound heads on the synchronizer and fed into this reader, where it is translated into sounds that we can understand and amplified so we may hear it. It is also called a "squawk box."

Sounding : The process of transferring sound onto a magnetic-striped 35mm picture print.

Spacing : See Fill.

Split Reel : A take-up reel which can be unscrewed into two sides. A core is placed inside and, after the sides have been screwed back together again, it can be used as a regular take-up reel. Since flatbed editing machines use film wound on cores, rather than on reels, this permits easy manipulation and projection of film cut on a flatbed without having to wind it all off the cores and onto take-up reels.

Spotting Session : A meeting in which the director, composer, editor, and music editor determine exactly where the scoring for the film shall fall.

Sprockets : The teeth on the film driving mechanism. These teeth link up with the sprocket holes on the film, those tiny perforations at the edge of the film, and transport the film forward at a designated rate. 35mm film has four sprocket holes for each frame, 16 mm film has only one, 70 mm has five.

Squawk Box : See Sound Reader.

Squeezed Image : See Anamorphic.

Steenbeck : A brand name for a common flatbed editing machine.

Streamer : A long line, usually three feet in length, drawn on the film to cue someone, either for an actor or actress, to let them know that a line to be looped is coming up, or a conductor to let him or her know that a musical cue is upcoming.

Stripe : 35mm track that contains one location for sound. Oxide has been glued onto part of a piece of clear 35mm film. In order for the track to take up correctly on reels, another, thinner, stripe is also glued onto the top of the film. It is called the "balance stripe" and is usually not recorded onto.

Striping : The act of gluing a thin layer of oxide onto the 35 mm picture. Later on, sound will be transferred onto it in a process called "sounding."

Superimposition : Also called a super. An optical in which one image is seen at the same time as another.

Sync : The condition when the sound and the picture that was taken on the set line up in the manner in which the events actually occurred during the shooting.

Synchronizer : A machine which has several rotating wheels with sprockets on them. By placing pieces of film or soundtrack on these wheels these pieces can be run in perfect sync with each other.

Sync Point : Any visual or aural place in the film which can be used to find the sync between the two. The normal sync point is the slate.

Tail Trim : See Trim.

Take : The single recording of a set-up. If take one is not satisfactory to the director he will do take two, then take three, until he is satisfied. The next set-up will start with take one again.

Take-Up Reel : A metal or plastic reel on which film is stored.

Timing : The act of correcting the color balance of the individual takes in the cut negative. Each shot must be balanced individually so that the slight differences between them can be evened out. Also called "color-correcting" or "balancing."

Transfer : A sound copy. After a day's shooting, the sound is on 1/4 inch tape. It is then transferred onto mag stock for use in editing.

Trim : A piece of a take which is left over after a portion of that take has been cut out and used in the cut of the film. A piece which comes before the section used in the film is called a "head trim," a portion after the section used is called a "tail trim."

Trim Bin : A large barrel into which takes of film are hung. They are usually rectangular and lined with a felt-like material to prevent the film from scratching as it hangs down into the pin from a rack of pins above it. Also called a "trim barrel."

Trim Tabs : See Cinetabs.

Unit : See Element.

Virgin Stock : Soundtrack stock onto which no sound has yet been recorded.

Walla : A background sound effect of a crowd murmuring.

Wild Sound : See Wild Track.

Wild Track : Sound recorded on the set with no accompanying picture. Also called "wild sound."

Work Picture : The cut-together film. Also called the "cut" or "cut picture."

Zeroing Out : Setting the synchronizer, moviola, or flatbed footage counter to zero.

VOCABULARY

Aspect ratio : The relationship of screen width to height. There are four ratios. "Standard" ratio existed from the early 1930s through the early 1950s and is 1:1.3. Two wise-screen ratios are 1:1.6 and 1:1.85.

Auteur : French term for the film director who places a personal style on his or her films.

Avant-garde : Often used to explain works of artists that are personal, experimental, and not aimed at a wide audience.

Backlighting : Lights from behind the characters that set them off from the background.

Chiaroscuro : A term from art history that refers to the use of deep shadow in the mise-en-scene.

Cinema verite : A version of documentary developed by the French in the late fifties and sixties that attempted to capture the ongoingness of everyday life without narration.

Cinematographer (director of photography) : Working with a film's director, the cinematographer lights the scene, chooses the appropriate lenses and film stock, and therefore carries a large responsibility for determining the look of a film.

Classical Hollywood style : The classical Hollywood style refers to a complex collection of formal and thematic elements that became basic to Hollywood filmmaking by the early teens. Continuity cutting - including shot/reverse shot and over-the-shoulder cutting - the 180-degree rule, happy endings, psychologically motivated characters, villains getting punished, women becoming wives and mothers are all associated with the classical Hollywood style. The continuity style is a subset of the classical Hollywood style.

Close-up	:	The actor's face fills the screen. Also, medium close-up, where the actor is seen from the upper torso.
Composition	:	The arrangement of characters and surroundings within the boundaries of the screen frame.
Continuity style/ Continuity Editing	:	Smooth, seamless editing that links shots so that the cuts appear invisible to the viewer.
Cultural studies	:	A wise-ranging critical approach to works of imagination that examines them in light of the cultures they are part of and that create them.
Culture	:	The sum total of the intricate ways we relate to ourselves, our peers, our community, our country, world and universe.
Deep focus	:	In deep-focus cinematography, all objects from front to rear of the composition are in sharp focus.
Documentary	:	A film that records actual events, often creating dramatic impact through editing.
Editing	:	The process of cutting film footage and assembling the pieces into an expressive, narrative structure.
Editor	:	The person who assembles the shots of a film into its final shape.

Establishing shot : Before a cutting pattern can begin, there must be a shot that establishes the whole space. Examples of establishing shots are the initial two-shot of characters in a dialogue sequence, or the image of an entire roomful of people, or of the city in which the film takes place.

Expressionist : This term originally referred to the style of film and theater in post-World War I Germany, where the mise-en-scene expressed the exaggerated, neurotic psychological state of the characters. Now it is used to refer to a mise-en-scene that is dark, distorted, and menacing.

Fill lighting : Lights that fill in the scene, creating accents, removing or adding shadow.

Film noir : A genre of film developed in the 1940s. Noir has a literary heritage in the hard-boiled detective fiction of Raymond Chandler and Dashiell Hammett and the novels of James M. Cain. Its cinematic lineage is German Expressionism and Welles' Citizen Kane. It is marked by a mise-en-scene of heavy shadow and narratives of weak men destroyed by predatory women.

Flow : A notion developed by the British cultural scholar Raymond Williams to define the ways that disparate and incoherent elements, commercials, promotions, and the shows themselves move together seamlessly on television.

Frankfurt school : Short for the Frankfurt Institute for Social Research, founded in Germany in 1924, much of it devoted to the study of popular culture and its productions.

Genre : A "kind" of story or narrative, made up of character types, plot lines, and settings common to all its members. Science fiction films and Westerns are genres, for example.

High-keyed lighting: Creates a bright, evenly lit scene.

Intertextuality : The way texts are interwoven or refer to each other in film, music, and the other arts. "Sampling" in rap is a kind of intertextuality.

Italian neorealism : Developed by the Italians at the end of World War II, a genre that defied studio conventions by filming on the streets, using nonprofessional or semi-professional actors to define a working class ruined by the war.

Jump cut	The result of editing out unnecessary transitions so that continuity is replaced by rapid changes in space.
Key light	The main overhead light that lights the faces and is reflected in the eyes.
Long shot (long takes)	Characters and surroundings are shown at the considerable distance from the camera.
Medium close-up	Character is shown from the shoulders up.
Medium shot	Character is shown from the waist up.
Melodrama	With comedy, the major genre of film, providing large arcs of emotion, often spilling into the music and mise-en-scene, and ending with the death of a beloved character or a closure in heterosexual marriage.
Mise-en-scene	The use of space within the frame: the placement of actors and props, the relationship of the camera to the space in front of it, camera movement, the use of color or black and white, lighting, the size of the screen frame itself.
Montage	A style of editing that juxtaposes shots to build dramatic tension. Sergei Eisenstein used montage as the basic structure of his films.

Over-the-shoulder cutting pattern : A major component of the classical Hollywood style. A dialogue sequence (two people talking to each other) begins with a two-shot of the participants and then proceeds to cut from over-the-shoulder of one speaker to over-the-shoulder of another. Occasionally a shot of one of the participants talking or listening with be cut into the pattern.

Pan : The camera pivots on its tripod or dolly. A pan an be lateral (side to side) or up and down.

Panning and scanning : The only way to show the entire width of a wise-screen film on television is to matte the top and bottom of the screen with black bars (the process is called letter-box format). Because many people believe they are seeing less of the film in this format (they are actually seeing more), television broadcasters and videotape distributors blow up the image to a square and move the focus around in that image to find what they think are the important elements.

Point of view : Simply, the representation of what a character sees. But it also refers to the dominant "voice" of the film, the teller of the film, similar to third-person point of view in fiction.

Post-studio period : Since the late fifties, when the studios no longer controlled every aspect of a film's production.

Producer : The individual who administers the making of an entire film, and often puts together its financing.

Production designer: Conceives and elaborates the setting's rooms and exteriors that help give a film its visual texture.

Reverse shot : Cutting to the opposite side of the previous shot. In a dialogue scene, a reverse shot occurs when a cut is made from over the shoulder of one character to over the shoulder of the other character. If a character is seen looking at something and a cut is made to what she is looking at, that is a reverse shot.

Screwball comedy : Films of the 1930s in whih both members of a romantic - often married - couple carried equal weight with dialogue of wit, strength, and self-possession.

Shot : An unedited, or uncut, length of film.

Shot/reverse shot : Any pair of shots in which the second shot reveals what is on the other side of the previous shot. If, for example, the first shot is a hat and the second shot is a character looking at something, the character constitutes the reverse shot and we assume that character is looking at the hat.

Silent era : From the beginning of film to the late 1920s, there was no recorded sould accompanying the image. Nonetheless, films were never shown without sound. A piano or, in a big movie palace, an entire symphony orchestra played a score that was often created especially for a particular film.

Studio system : Beginning in the early 1920s , the film studios developed a production process --with the producer at the head on any given film—and a style of shooting and edition that, despite many variations, remains to this day.

Take : A shot made during the production of a film. A scene in a film is the result of editorial choices made from many differing takes.

Technicolor : A proprietary color process that used three strips of black and white film, each one exposed to either red, blue, or yellow light. These strips were then used to transfer color dye to impart a rich color to film that did not fade with age.

The New Wave : A group of French filmmakers - Jean-Luc Godard, Claude Chabrol, Francois Truffaut, Eric Rohmer, Jacque Rivette - who started as film critics, became filmmakers in the late-fifties, and briefly revolutionized the look of cinema.

Two-shot : A shot composed of two people.

EFFECTS RESEARCH: GLOSSARY

Actuality : The term used in the media to refer to footage/film/tape of events as they happen. Semioticians see actuality as a key device for anchoring the preferred reading on the supposed 'facts' presented 'as they happened'.

Agenda setting : The committee of, say, the local union branch will set the agenda for the next branch meeting. The agenda shows the order in which items are to be discussed and anything not on the agenda is not discussed. In a similar way, the media are said to perform an agenda-setting rôle, both determining what is a matter for public debate and determining the order of importance of such matters. Further, the media are said to set the framework for debate on current issues.

Anchorage : A term used by Barthes to describe the interaction of words and visual texts. A photograph, according to Barthes is polysemic (i.e. open to a range of possible meanings). Ordinarily text is added, perhaps in the form of a caption or an advertising slogan, to 'anchor' the meaning, to lead the reader towards the preferred reading of the visual text. More broadly, anchorage of an image's meaning can occur not only through words, but, say, through the juxtaposition of two images.

Bardic television : A term introduced by Fiske and Hartley (1978) to emphasize the active and productive signifying work done by television. Rather than merely 'reflecting' society, television, similarly to the rôle played by Celtic bards, mediate between the rulers and patrons who pay them on the one hand and society as a whole on the other. In this way, the bard (television), once its rôle is established, has an important function in dealing with social change and conflict. It determines what is within the bounds of common sense and what is outside it (see ideology).

Catharsis (or cathartic effect) : The idea originated with the ancient Greek philosopher,

Aristotle, who believed that the experience of watching tragedy is cathartic, i.e. it purges the spectator of certain strong emotions. As a result mainly of experiments by Feshbach and Singer, this idea has been developed in media effects research. Watching aggressive media output, it is proposed, does not make viewers more aggressive; quite the contrary - since the vicarious aggression experienced through the media purges the viewer of aggression, the result of watching violence is less aggression. The same argument is sometimes adduced in defence of pornography. Some researchers have taken the example of Japan, where there is far more violent sex in the media than in Europe, yet a much lower incidence of violent sex crime, to support the view that media experience can be cathartic.

Centre for Contemporary Cultural Studies (Birmingham) : Most of the media theories which emerged from the Birmingham centre were in the Marxist' critical' or 'radical' tradition of research. In Birmingham the concentration was on ideological control of the media, especially the way that media practi-tioners relied on powerful groups and institutions and unconsciously internalized the values of that dominant culture. The best known representative of this approach is probably Stuart Hall.

Centre for Mass Communication Research (Leicester) : Examination of media effects, mostly in the Marxist 'critical' tradition of research. Leicester placed the emphasis primarily on economic considerations, such as ownership and the effects of the media market, as well as on indirect influence form the state. The best known representative of the Leicester approach is probably Murdock.

Closure : (1) In Gestalt psychology the term refers to the way that we fill in gaps where there is missing information in a stimulus.

(2) In the analysis of texts, the term refers to ideological closure, which means the strategies used in the text to lead the reader to make sense of the text according to a particular ideological framework. The idea of ideological closure is useful because it leads us to examine how a text has been constructed to lead to a particular reading and exclude other possible readings.

Consensus : The word means a generally shared agreement. The term is used in particular by Marxist critics of the media, who argue that the media operate to create a consensus in society (or at least an illusion of consensus) that the norms, laws and rules in our society are the only 'right' ones, which any right-thinking member of our society must accept. Thus, for example, those who might operate outside the consensus, such as union 'activists' or 'terrorists' do not normally have their ideas and views presented by the media as if they are 'reasonable'. In order to strengthen the consensus the media periodically whip up moral panics against those deviants ('folk devils') who are deemed to lie outside the central cultural system, e.g. 'welfare scroungers', 'union activists', 'travellers', 'ravers' etc. (See also ideology).

Conspiracy theory : With particular reference to the mass media, this view assumes that a small and powerful, and often hidden, élite are able to use the mass media to condition and persuade passive audiences into conforming to the powerful élite's wishes. It depends very much on the notion of all-powerful media and easily duped audiences. It is difficult to find evidence that the media really are that powerful and 'conspiracy theory' is often dismissed because you would otherwise sound like some kook who takes the X-Files literally. Nevertheless, it's something close to this that underlies much left-wing criticism of the media.

Construction of reality : In media studies, this idea emphasizes that there is no single 'reality', rather a range of definitions of 'reality'. Reality as presented by the mass media is therefore not a picture or reflection of 'reality', but, rather, a constructed interpretation of reality. In the view of 'radical' critics of the media in particular, the mass media play a crucial rôle in 'constructing reality' for the rest of us. In the view of many representatives of post-structuralism and post-modernism, just about every aspect of reality seems to be considered a social construction.

Content analysis : The statistical analysis of a range of texts. The results are usually compared with a different set of results from the same range of texts - e.g. what proportion of reports about men in the tabloid press represents men as victims and what proportion represents women as victims?—or with some 'objective' standard, such as official statistics—e.g. what proportion of women in soaps is shown as housewives as against the proportion of women in the population who are housewives The most serious problem with content analysis is the initial selection of categories. The second most serious problem is where to find your objective standard.

Copycat effect : Also referred to as contagion effect or imitation effect - the supposed power of the media to create an 'epidemic' of behaviour based on that witnesses in the media. The idea is by no means new; the eighteenth century novel Die Leiden des jungen Werther by the great German writer Goethe, was accused of having led to a wave of suicides amongst the young. More recently, the media have been blamed for the 1981 riots which hit British cities; later in the eighties, for a spate of prison rioting; in the early nineties, police in Wales asked the media not to report details of suicides involving carbon monoxide poisoning from exhaust fumes because they believed that suicides were imitating the suicides in press reports; in

1999, doctors researching the effect of medical soaps reported that after a 1996 episode of Casualty portraying with a paracetamol overdose actual cases rose by 20% and doubled amongst people who had seen the episode (source British Medical Journal, reported in The Guardian, April 9 1999. It seems to be generally agreed amongst media researchers that it is very difficult to find any clear evidence for the copycat effect, but the doctors in the BMA study were firmly convinced. One of them , Christopher Bulstrode, Professor of Orthopaedics at the John Radcliffe Hospital in Oxford, commented: "We were expecting a fall in overdoses because it was a horrid scene. What we got was a 20% increase, and we were gobsmacked. One of the reasons we have been so slow in publishing was we didn't believe it. We have gone back over and over and over again. It really happened."

Cultural dopes : The view that the readers of media texts are the more or less willing dupes of the media producers. This view is now not widely accepted, since greater emphasis is placed by media researchers on the active meaning-producing work of readers. A more 'modern' view of audiences is presented by Fiske.

A homogeneous, externally produced culture cannot be sold ready-made to the masses: culture simply does not work like that. Nor do the people behave or live like the masses, an aggregation of alienated, one-dimensional persons whose only consciousness is false, whose only relationship to the system that enslaves them is one of unwitting (if not willing) dupes. Popular culture is made by the people, not produced by the culture industry. All the culture industries can do is produce a repertoire of texts or cultural resources for the various formations of the people to use or reject in the ongoing process of producing their popular culture. (Fiske (1989)).

Cultural imperialism : Cultural imperialism or media imperialism is the thesis that 'Western' (especially American) cultural values are being forced on non-Western societies, to which they are spread most especially by the mass media. Herbert Schiller argues forcefully that the US-inspired spread of 'free trade' and 'free speech' since the Second World

War has, in view of the imbalance of economic power, worked to the advantage of the US. He quotes a number of official sources which make it clear that the establishment of US economic, military and cultural hegemony was deliberate US policy, which would depend crucially on US dominance of global communications. Schiller argues that the (mostly US-based) transnational media and communications corporations which now span the globe have reached the point where they pose a distinct threat to the sovereignty of the weaker nation-states. Clearly the US are dominant in the export of media products, as well as in the control of news agencies, and, even where the US originals are not purchased, the genres of US TV are closely copied. However, recent reception studies suggest that we cannot simply deduce the acceptance of American values from the prevalence of US media products.

Deregulation : The process of removing or diluting the rules which govern the operation of certain companies or areas of industry. In the media, this refers especially to the move, in western Europe, away from state-regulated broadcasting systems towards systems which are more open to market forces.

Desensitization : Some theorists argue that the constant media diet of violence desensitizes audiences (makes them less sensitive) to real human suffering. It is hard to find proof for the theory, though the practice of systematic desensitization in behaviour modification may lend incidental support to the theory.

Belson's 1978 study of over 1500 teenage boys did not find any support at all for the desesitization hypothesis. The effect of the 'distant violence' presented in the news was virtually nill and the effect of directly experienced violence was even slightly negative, which, if anything, suggests increased sensitization to real-world violence.

Deviance : Deviance is a form of behaviour which is considered to violate society's norms and therefore to be unacceptable. Many critics of the media would argue that the apparent consensus as regards those norms is in part manufactured by the media by the process of labelling certain groups' or individuals' behaviour as deviant and then duly reacting to it with moral outrage on behalf of 'ordinary, decent people'. Thus the media serve to legitimate the dominant ideology, which in fact serves the interests of the powerful groups in society.

Deviance amplification : The process whereby activity labelled as deviant is 'amplified' by a broad reaction in society which is co-ordinated mainly by the mass media. The development is seen more or less as a spiral: the initial behaviour is labelled 'devinat'; information is relayed from primary definers to the media and thence to the wider society; there is a negative social reaction; consequently, the deviant groups become isolated and react by resisting the consensus view and possibly becoming more actively deviant; the increased 'deviance' leads to increased social control and at this point the whole spiral starts all over again.

Discourse : Not an easy term to get to grips with, partly because it is used differently in different subject areas.

In linguistics the term is commonly used to refer to an utterance larger than a single sentence.

In interpersonal communication, 'discourse analysis' refers to the analysis of the verbal and non-verbal aspects of an interaction; it analyses the verbal and non-verbal rules and conventions which apply, as well as the context in which the interaction takes place, the content of the utterances etc. Discourse analysis often forms a part of ethnographic studies.

In cultural studies, the term is generally thought of as having been most usefully developed by the French post-structuralist philosopher Michel Foucault. While here the analysis of discourse is concerned with the meanings of language and other codes, the focus is primarily on the power relationships embodied in those codes. Codes and their meanings do not stand somehow outside society and history; rather they are always subject to the historical and social context of the time and prevailing power relationships and conflicts, each discourse being a limited range of possible statements, by that very limitation defining what it is possible and not possible to say. Some discourses are considered more 'legitimate' than others, these others receiving little recognition. Thus, there are the discourses of, say, radio and television news, the discourses of medicine, science, academia and so on. In society there is a constant ideological struggle between discourses; for example, the discourse of free-market capitalism is now dominant, hegemonic, whereas the discourse of Marxism is defined as irrelevant.

Discourse is a language or system of representation that has developed socially in order to make and circulate a coherent set of meanings about an important topic area. These meanings serve the interests of that section of society within which the discourse originates and which works ideologically to naturalize those meanings into common sense. .... Discourse is thus a social act which may promote or oppose the dominant ideology, and is thus often referred to as a 'discursive practice'. Any account of a discourse or a discursive practice must include its topic area, its social origin and its ideological work: we should not, therefore, think about a discourse of economics, or of gender, but of a capitalist (or socialist) discourse of economics, or the patriarchal (or feminist) discourse of gender. Such discourse frequently become institutionalized, particularly by the media industries, in so far as they are structured by a socially produced set of conventions that are tacitly accepted by both industry and consumers. In this sense we can talk about the discourse of news, or of advertising.

Empirical : The adjective 'empirical' means 'based upon experience'. In philosophy the term empiricism refers to the theory that all concepts are derived from experience and that all statements which express knowledge must ultimately derive their justification from experience; those who hold that view are referred to as empiricists.

Essentialism : Is most commonly understood as a belief in the real, true essence of things, the invariable and fixed properties which define the 'whatness' of a given entity.... Importantly, essentialism is typically defined in opposition to difference. . . . The opposition is a helpful one in that it reminds us that a complex system of cultural, social, psychical, and historical differences, and not a set of preexistent human essences, position and constitute the subject. However, the binary articulation of essentialism and difference can also be restrictive, even obfuscating, in that it allows us to ignore or deny the differences within essentialism.

The condemnation of 'essentialism' by commentators often described as post-modernists has, I think, performed important work in clearing away the cultural accretions around concepts which we use unthinkingly in everyday life without being aware of the cultural baggage which attaches to them. Potentially an essentialist approach to almost any concept is totalizing and fascist. America is essentially white, Anglophone and committed to free enterprise and democracy. Women are essentially caring, nurturing and emotional. It is readily apparent how such essentialism obscures difference and can work to serve the interests of those who fall within the essentialist definition of Americans, women or whomever.

However, 'essentialism/essentialist' seems in some quarters to have become a blanket term of abuse, itself totalizing and fascist. I would have thought it possible to define a triangle as having three sides and three angles which add up to 180 degrees without fear of contradiction, but I wouldn't be surprised to find that there's someone out there who will condemn me as essentialist for doing so.

In the sciences, essentialism is tantamount to creationism. In the humanities, the label implies that the person subscribes to insane beliefs such as that the sexes are not socially constructed, there are universal emotions, a real world exists and so on. And in the social sciences, 'essentialism' has joined 'reductionism', 'determinism', and 'reification' as a term of abuse hurled at anyone who tries to explain human thought and behaviour rather than describe it.

In the postmodernist or poststructuralist lexicon, the terms "essentialism" and "foundationalism" are used to denote a host of presumably bad attitudes, including the view that interpretation or theory can and should be judged in relation to some reality external to itself, the view that some social groups have characteristics or interests that are given rather than continually constructed and reconstructed—and reductionism, stereotyping, as in the view that all women are nurturent, or that African Americans have innate musical abilities. The fact that the term essentialism refers simultaneously to an epistemological approach and also to racist, sexist or at least naive politics tends to link these two and makes it difficult to have a calm discussion of whether there is such a thing as truth, and whether theory should be judged by reality external to itself. In many discussions the use of the term "essentialist" is enough to identify the philosophical stance as politically retrograde and therefore unacceptable.

Ex-nomination : The term coined by Roland Barthes to refer to the way in which the bourgeoisie remains 'anonymous' by succeeding in presenting its ideology to us as 'common sense'.

Folk devils and moral panics According to Cohen, certain groups periodically become the focus of moral panics. They are labelled as being outside the central core values of our consensual society and as posing a particular threat to them. The groups investigated by Cohen were the Mods and Rockers - today, New Age Travellers or those who attend raves could be seen as their modern equivalent. The 'central core values' which such groups transgress against are argued to be the norms and values which primarily serve the interests of the dominant classes. The media, in particular the press, whip up a moral panic which is coupled with calls for strengthening the forces of law and order. According to this view the Criminal Justice Act 1994, with its legislation specifically targetting travellers and raves, is the response to the moral panic in the media.

Fourth estate : This term appears sometimes to be used to refer to the 'three powers' in a modern democratic society, at other times to refer to the three 'estates' in pre-revolutionary France. As you will see, it amounts to the same thing either way.

Gatekeeping : The selection or rejection of events in the 'real' world. For example, an editor decides on what's going to be covered, an organizer briefs the camera crews, the reporter decides what 'angle' the story will be covered from and so on. These people are all gatekeepers. The concept of gatekeeping tends to be related to rather mechanistic models of communication processes. Though it may serve to remind us of the operation of a selection process in the representation of news, it is essentially too simplistic to be a great deal of use.

Glasgow University Media Group : Produces very influential research into the operation of ideology in the broadcast media under the titles Bad News, More Bad News, Really Bad News. The authors attacked the perceived view that broadcast news is less partial and more 'objective' than other news sources. Their findings were vehemently attacked by the broadcasters themselves, but are frequently used as sources by other academic critics of the media.

Hegemony : In the writings of Gramsci, hegemony refers to the dominance of one social class over others. The term bourgeois cultural hegemony is also used - it refers to the dominance of the bourgeoisie over other classes, but the key word is cultural, as it emphasises that it is the bourgeois culture, with all the beliefs, values and norms which it incorporates, that is dominant. A more traditional Marxist view would place the emphasis rather on the economic control exerted by the dominant class.

In the Gramscian view, the bourgeoisie are successful in projecting their view of the world as 'natural' and 'common sense', 'taken for granted', 'legitimate', although in fact it serves only their interests. Their view becomes the consensus view.

Hegemony is potentially always threatened. It can only be maintained by the consent of the subordinate classes. The subordinate can pose a challenge to hegemony and the consensus may be broken. Society is seen therefore as a constant struggle between ideologies competing for hegemony.

The media, from this viewpoint, are seen as playing a vital rôle in constructing the consensus.

Hierarchy of access : The media rarely give first-hand accounts of 'deviants'' behaviour. Their behaviour is explained for us by others. The behaviour of such groups is often reported in the press, but they have little or no control over what is said:

In any system of ranked groups, participants take it as given that members of the highest group have the right to define the way things really are .... those at the top have access to a more complete picture of what is going on than anybody else. Members of lower groups will have incomplete information and their view of reality will be partial and distorted in consequence.

The 'accessed voices' ... speak from a limited range of social positions, usually those contained within the safe limits of parliamentary democracy. Voices that appear too radical are not allowed to speak directly, but are reported, that is, mediated, if their point of view is represented at all.

Ideological State Apparatus (ISA) : The term used by the French Marxist philosopher Althusser to refer to those agencies of the state which act to communicate to us the dominant ideology and persuade us to internalize it. These are distinguished by Althusser from the RSAs (Repressive State Apparatuses) such as the police, military, penal system and legislature. ISAs include the education system, the family, the legal system. the party-political system, culture and the mass media.

Ideology : A system of ideas and beliefs. In Communication studies, the term is often used to refer to a 'dominant ideology'. The idea derives from Karl Marx's use of the term to apply to any system of thought which upholds the position of the dominant class: 'In every historical epoch the dominant ideas are those of the ruling classes.'

Interpellation/ appellation/ hailing / audience positioning : This term (or any of its synonyms) is taken from the French philosopher, Louis Althusser. It is the process whereby ideology 'hails' an individual as its subject; a 'subject-position' is constructed for the audience member by the way in which the text interpellates him/her. Thus, for example, the discourse of free-market capitalism interpellates the subject as the rational, self-interested consumer of classical economics.

Intertextuality : Any text depends on a host of prior conventions, codes, other texts. The term is sometimes used to refer to the unavoidable multiplicity of references in any text (see also infinite semiosis below); sometimes it is used to refer to deliberate references, quotations or pastiches. In the first of these senses, the intertext of Independence Day includes all other films featuring alien attack, the Prince of Bel-Air, Hollywood blockbusters foregrounding special effects etc. In the second sense, The Untouchables features a conscious quotation from the Odessa Steps sequence in Eisenstein's Battleship Potemkin, Brian de Palma's Dressed to Kill features a series of conscious references to Hitchcock's Psycho etc. I have also seen the term hypertextuality used to refer to example such as the latter two, as well as pastiches (e.g. Gentlemen Wear Plaid's pastiche of film noir) and remakes.

Knowledge gap : The knowledge gap hypothesis states that 'as the infusion of mass media information into a social system increases, segments of the population with higher socio-economic status tend to acquire this information at a faster rate than the lower status segments, so that the gap in knowledge between these segments tends to increase rather than decrease' (Tichenor et al. (1970) quoted in Kleinnijenhuis (1991))

Labelling : Term associated with Howa Becker, whose study 196 Tl Outsiders: studies in tl sociology of deviancy consid how certain people and th things they do or think come t be labelled as 'deviant'. Hi study shows how the powerfu groups in society use th 'labelling process' to define wha is acceptable and whos 'deviant' behaviour lies outsid the domain of the acceptable (See also consensus and folk devils)

Mass society theory : The view that the mass media address a mass audience who are doped by the media. This view of the media audience (in the singular) as a passive, undifferentiated mass informs the hypodermic needle model media effects, as well as some aspects of the concern with cultural effects (see for example Adorno and Horkheimer).

Media Monitoring Group : Recently revived, having become inactive during the early 1990s, the Media Monitoring Group is closely associated with the Conservative Party. It appears to monitor the broadcast media for 'socialist' bias, its findings being used to support Conservative politicians' sporadic attacks on broadcasters in the UK.

Medium is the message : One of those obscure sayings of the 60s media guru Marshall McLuhan. McLuhan argues that no medium is neutral and what is said is profoundly affected by the medium in which it is said. The saying may also be taken to imply, in a sense, that the medium is 'more important' than the message. If interpreted in this way, then the saying can be seen to be close to the contemporary post-modern pre-occupation with the over-production of signs, the superficiality of media communication and the 'implosion of meaning' (Baudrillard).

Moral entrepreneurs: The term is used by sociologist Howard Becker to refer to those campaigners who create new rules for the rest of us, such as Mary Whitehouse of National VALA: "The existing rules do not satisfy him because there is some evil which profoundly disturbs him. He feels that nothing can be right in the world until rules are made to correct it. He operates with an absolute ethic; what he sees is truly and absolutely evil with no qualification. Any means is justified to do away with it. The crusader is fervent and righteous, often self-righteous.' (Becker (1963) pp. 147-8).

Multi-accentuality : The polysemy of signs, i.e. their capacity to signify more than one meaning. The notion is particularly useful for the investigation of the way that signs which may at first appear neutral are in fact ideologically loaded, e.g. he, man, mankind etc. identified by feminist critics.

News management : This term is normally used to describe the way that individuals or organizations attempt to control the flow of news to the media and to 'set the agenda' for the media. This might involve issuing a press release which is embargoed, holding press conferences times to make the lunch-time and early-evening news, or staging an event which is big enough or unusual enough to grab the media's attention.

Pluralism : In media studies a view of the mass media as enjoying a considerable degree of independence from the state, political parties and pressure groups. They are seen as being in the control of autonomous managers who allow media professionals a great deal of freedom. In this view, audiences are not seen as manipulated by the media as the audiences are considered to enter into the relationship with the media on equal terms. Broadly speaking the media are seen as offering a wide selection of the views of various groups in society. This view should be contrasted with those of radical researchers.

News values : The criteria which journalists and editors use to determine whether or not an event is 'newsworthy'.

Pluralist : The pluralist view of the mass media sees them as important agencies within a free and democratic society. Media institutions are seen as being free, by and large, of any government control and thus free to present whatever point of view they want, audience members beng free to choose whatever 'line' suits them in a 'pick 'n' mix' approach to media definitions of reality.

Polysemy : All signs are polysemic, i.e. capable of having a range of possible meanings. The range of meanings is narrowed down by the context. A photographic image is inherently polysemic. Its meaning is anchored by accompanying text.

Preferred reading (or dominant reading) : Semiologists have sometimes made a distinction between open and closed texts. All texts are open to a variety of possible readings, but in a 'closed' text one particular reading is clearly preferred to others. Closed texts are associated with mass culture and thus include most mass media texts. The preferred reading of the text (also referred to as 'dominant reading') is the reading intended by the text.

Stuart Hall uses the .term 'preferred reading' in Cohen and Young (1981) in his discussion of the presentation of the way that the possible meanings of news photographs are closed off by cropping, anchorage by captions, juxtaposition and so on. However, Hall also accepts the possibility that certain readers of media texts will arrive at a negotiated reading, where the dominant values and current social structures are broadly accepted, but the readers will nevertheless be prepared to argue that some groups are treated unfairly within those structures. Yet others will arrive at an oppositional reading where the preferred reading is wholly rejected.

In part, Hall's view of these three types of reading answers a criticism that the radical critics do not pay sufficient attention to what the audience actually do with texts. However,

Hall's (1980) preferred reading theory was an early attempt to account for the process by which popular readers could make their meanings out of the text, but it still assumed that they engaged with the whole text in the way that the text itself 'wanted'. The readings preferred by the dominant ideology were structured into the text as a whole, and they could be resisted or negotiated with only in terms of an engagement with this complete text.

Press barons : The death of Lord Northcliffe (owner of The Times, The Daily Mail and others) in 1922, left Lords Rothermere, Beaverbrook, Camrose and Kemsley free to establish a dominant position. By 1937, they owned nearly one in two national and local daily papers in the UK, and one in every three Sunday papers. Combined circulation was over 13 million. They were open about their use of newspapers for political propaganda. Beaverbrook told the Royal Commission on the Press that he ran The Daily Express 'merely for the purpose of making propaganda and with no other motive.' This attitude led Prime Minister Baldwin to say, 'what the proprietorship of these papers is aiming at is power, and power without responsibility - the prerogative of the harlot throughout the ages.'

Primary definers : The powerful groups in society who have greater access to the media and therefore a greater influence over the media's definition of 'reality'. For comment on crime, for example, the media will consult police and Home Office spokespersons, for comment on economic policy, they will consult politicians and 'independent City analysts'. Such people are 'primary definers'.

Propaganda model : The view, formulated from a political economic perspective on the media, especially associated with Noam Chomsky that the media 'serve to mobilize support for the special interests that dominate the state and private activity' (Chomsky & Herman (1988 p. xi). For Chomsky there is no essential difference between the American (and European) news media and those of totalitarian countries. Chomsky's Necessary Illusions (1989) presents a devastating account of the propaganda function of the American media, not so much by the sophistication of the argument, but by the wealth of the evidence he produces of the American media parroting government policy. The underlying premise is really quite simple, neatly and powerfully encapsulated in the following three quotations:

Those segments of the media that can reach a substantial audience are major corporations and are closely integrated with even larger conglomerates. Like other businesses, they sell a product to buyers. Their market is advertisers, and the 'product' is audiences, with a bias towards more wealthy audiences, which improve advertising rates. [....] In short, the major media - particularly, the élite media that set the agenda that others generally follow - are corporations 'selling' privileged audiences to other businesses. It would hardly come as a surprise if the picture they present were to reflect the perspectives and interests of the sellers, the buyers and the product.

Case by case we find that conformity is the easy way, and the path to privilege and prestige; dissidence carries personal costs that may be severe, even in a society that lacks such means of control as death squads, psychiatric prisons, or extermination camps. The very structure of the media is designed to induce conformity to established doctrine. In a three-minute stretch between commercials, or in seven hundred words, it is impossible to present unfamiliar thoughts or surprising conclusions with the argument and evidence require to afford them some credibility.

The model of media as corporate oligopoly is the natural system for capitalist democracy. It has, accordingly, reached its highest form in the most advanced of these societies, particularly the United States, where media concentration is high, public radio and television are limited in scope, and elements of the radical democratic model exist only at the margins, in such phenomena as listener-supported community radio and the alternative or local press, often with a noteworthy effect on the social and political culture and the sense of empowerment in the communities that benefit from these options. In this respect, the United States represents the form towards which capitalist democracy is tending; related tendencies include the progressive elimination of unions and other popular organizations that interfere withprivate power, an electoral system that is increasingly stage-managed as a public relations exercise, avoidance of welfare measures such as national health insurance that also impinge on the prerogatives of the privileged, and so on.

Public interest : Matters are defined by the Press Complaints Commission as being in the public interest (and therefore an exception to the prohibitions of the PCC's Code) if they are a matter of i) detecting or exposing crime or a serious misdemeanour ii) protecting public health and safety iii) preventing the public from being misled by some statement or action of an individual or organization. In any matters raising issues beyond these definitions, the PCC requires a full explanation by the editor of the publication concerned.

Public service broadcasting : A term which is not easy to define. The essential notion here is that broadcasting's function is not simply to satisfy commercial interests by giving the public what they want in an attempt to maximize audience figures, but, rather, to inform, educate and entertain the public, the notion of 'quality' being central. Examples are: that broadcasters are legally required to be impartial in their coverage of news and current affairs; that broadcasters must carry a certain proportion of educational programmes; that broadcasters must broadcast a certain proportion of current affairs during prime time - and so on.

Radical : In media studies, the 'radical' tradition is that which is more or less Marxist in its approach, seeing the media as playing an important rôle in the transmission of the dominant ideology. The approach was influenced by Marx, The Frankfurt School, Althusser and, later, Gramsci.

Readerly text : The translation of Barthes' lisible in his book S/Z an analysis of Balzac's Sarrasine. Barthes opposes this to the scriptible or 'writerly' text. The readerly text is seen as privileging the values sought and assumed in the classic text, for example a linear narrative, realism, whereas the writerly text stimulates the reader who is aware of the work of the text. Thus the reader (in the conventional sense), rather than being a mere passive reader of the text, becomes a writer or producer of the text, participating in its construction. S/Z is often seen as one of the foremost texts of post-structuralist criticism, in part because the notion of the writerly text introduces the notion of uncertainty, indeter-minacy, which are characteristic of post-structuralist approaches to meaning.

Reception-analysis : Research which focuses on the way that individuals make meanings for media messages. Reception analysis has some similarity with uses and gratifications research, but is much more likely to use an ethnographic approach involving in-depth interviews, participant observation etc. Reception analysis has developed particularly since the early to mid-1980s. It tends generally to be associated with the view that audiences are active and is generally associated with the notion of resistive readings of media texts, associated with Michel de Certeau.

Reflexivity : A term used to refer to foregrounding by a text of its own made-ness or constructedness. For those of you who study drama, this will be familiar as Brecht's 'alienation effect'. Brecht was concerned to avoid the 'swindle' involved in naturalistic theatre's pretence that the play 'happened' rather than 'was made'. It may be seen as a method of undermining the pretensions of bourgeois theatre, whose realism, by concealing its own workings, draws the spectator into the bourgeois ideology which is inscribed in its claims to represent common-sense reality itself. It is no doubt because of its anti-bourgeois intentions that we find it being frequently used in, for example, Godard's cinema. But it's no longer as simple as that (if it ever was): what do you make of Wayne and Garth talking to the camera in Wayne's World; or of the fact that every news interview or documentary foregrounds the cuts, no longer masking them with 'noddies'.

Rhetorical figures site : For definitions of some of the more obscure terminology of rhetoric.

Semiosis : Signification, the production of meaning; frequently used in the phrase infinite semiosis whereby one signifier refers only to another signifier, meaning constantly deferred in an infinite chain. This latter term tends to be associated with post-structuralism, one of the characteristics of which is the shift of emphasis from signified to signifier.

Semiotic guerrilla warfare : A term taken from Umberto Eco by John Fiske to describe the resistive tactics employed by subordinate groups in constructing counterhegemonic meanings for media texts. The term is particularly descriptive of the ideas popularized by de Certeau and Fiske and coming increasingly to the fore in recent years in reception analysis.

Socialization : The process whereby individuals are made aware of the behaviour that others expect of them as regards the norms, values and culture of their society. Agents of socialization include the family, school, friendship groups, religious institutions and the mass media.

Three powers : In a democratic society, power is in principle divided between the three 'powers': the legislative power that makes the laws (e.g. the US Congress); the executive power that makes executive decisions on a day-to-day basis (e.g. the US

President); the judiciary who interpret the laws (e.g. the US Supreme Court). These powers supposedly counterbalance one another. This system of 'checks and balances' works to ensure that none of the three powers becomes too strong. Thus, for example, the President can send troops to war, but the Congress can refuse to vote the budget to sustain the war; the Congress can pass a law, but the Supreme Court can rule it unconstitutional. In practice, things are not always so rosey, especially not in the UK where the government of the day normally has supreme legislative and executive power.

Three estates : In pre-revolutionary France the three estates were the aristocracy, the clergy and the tiers état (third estate) - not the 'people' as we would think of them today, but the bourgeoisie. In principle the French parliament consisted of these three estates, but was in practice rarely called together.

The media often argue that they constitute the fourth estate, watching for wrongdoings of the other three. The fourth estate argument certainly has some validity and press exposures have led to the establishment of the Nolan Committee to investigate standards in public life (1995). However, it is an argument which seems sometimes to be a feeble excuse for the media to pry into the private affairs of MPs, ministers, royalty and others. The argument that the media constitute a fourth estate is closely linked to Habermas's recently revived notion of the 'public sphere'.

Frankfurt School Institute for Social Research founded 1923. The School's members were Horkheimer, Adorno, Benjamin, Marcuse, and, more recently, Jürgen Habermas. The members of the school were exiled by the Nazis to the US and, with the exception of Marcuse, returned post-war.They were concerned to develop critical theory from the works of Karl Marx. They greatly developed the critique of the mass media in mass society (what they referred to as the culture industry) and their work is therefore at the root of much Marxist criticism of the mass media. As they saw it, the culture industry played a highly manipulative rôle in modern society and served to control or subvert oppositional consciousness, thus removing any threat to the dominant capitalist class.

Two-step Flow : The term used by Katz and Lazarsfeld to describe their observation that media messages flow from the media to opinion leaders to the rest of the audience. The important point is that their research demonstrated that media effects are mediated by the pattern of our social contacts. They concluded that the media have limited effects.

Uses and Gratifications : Approaches to the media emphasize the active use made of media by audience members to seek gratification of a variety of needs. The standard adage is that, where effects research asks 'what do the media do to audiences?', the uses and gratifications approach asks 'what do audiences do with the media?'. Audiences are said to use the media to gratify needs. The needs most commonly identified are: surveillance (i.e. monitoring what's going on in the world), personal relationships, personal identity and diversion (i.e. entertainment and escapism).

War of the Worlds : A sci-fi story by H G Wells. Adapted for radio by the young

Orson Welles, the story of the Martian invasion (suitably transferred to the USA) was spread across a series of mock news bulletins on American radio in1938. It caused widespread panic. According to some reports, around a quarter of the six million listeners believed what they heard; many who lived near the site of the supposed invasion fled from the area; many are said to have reported that they had actually seen the alien invaders.

THEORIES OF MASS COMMUNICATION

Agenda setting : Theory that argues that media may not tell us what to think but that media tell us what to think about.

Attitude change theory : Theory that explains how peopleís attitudes are formed, shaped, and changed and how those attitudes influence behavior.

Critical cultural theory : Idea that media operate primarily to justify and support the status quo at the expense of ordinary people.

Cultivation analysis: Idea that television ìcultivatesî or constructs a reality of the world that, although possibly inaccurate, becomes the accepted reality simply because we as a culture believe it to be the reality.

Cultural theory : The idea that meaning and therefore effects are negotiated by media and audiences as they interact in the culture.

Dependency theory : Idea that mediaís power is a function of audience membersí dependency on the media and their content.

Disinhibitory effects: In social learning theory, seeing a model rewarded for prohibited or threatening behavior increases the likelihood that the observer will perform that behavior.

Dissonance theory : Argues that people, when confronted by new information, experience a kind of mental discomfort, a dissonance; as a result, they consciously and subconsciously work to limit or reduce that discomfort through the selective processes.

Grand theory : A theory designed to describe and explain all aspects of a given phenomenon.

Hypodermic needle theory : Idea that media are a dangerous drug that can directly enter a personís system.

Identification : In social learning theory, a special form of imitation where observers do not exactly copy what they have seen but make a more generalized but related response.

Imitation : In social learning theory, the direct replication of an observed behavior.

Inhibitory effects : In social learning theory, seeing a model punished for a behavior reduces the likelihood that the observer will perform that behavior.

Limited effects theory : Medias' influence is limited by peopleís individual differences, social categories, and personal relationships.

Magic bullet theory : The mass society theory idea that media are a powerful killing force that directly penetrates a persons' system.

Mainstreaming : In cultivation analysis, televisionís ability to move people toward a common understanding of how things are..

Mass communication theories : Explanations and predictions of social phenomena relating mass communication to various aspects of our personal and cultural lives or social systems.

Mass society theory : The idea that media are corrupting influences; they undermine the social order, and average people are defenseless against their influence.

Middle-range theories : Ideas that explain or predict only limited aspects of the mass communication process.

Modeling : In social learning theory, learning through imitation and identification.

Neo-Marxist theory : The theory that people are oppressed by those who control the culture, the superstructure, as opposed to the base Frankfurt School media theory, centered in neo-Marxism, that valued serious art, viewing it's consumption as a means to elevate all people toward a better life; typical media fare was seen as pacifying ordinary people while repressing them.

News production Research : The study of how economic and other influences on the way news is produced distort and bias news coverage toward those in power.

Observational learning : In social learning theory, observers can acquire (learn) new behaviors simply by seeing those behaviors performed.

Opinion followers : People who receive opinion leadersí interpretations of media content; from two-step flow theory.

Opinion leaders : People who initially consume media content, interpret it in light of their own values and beliefs, and then pass it on to opinion followers; from two-step flow theory.

Paradigm : A theory that summarizes and is consistent with all known facts, fundamental, even radical rethinking of what people believe to be true for a given body of knowledge.

Product positioning: He practice in advertising of assigning meaning to a product based on who buys the product rather than on the product itself.

Reinforcement theory : Joseph Klapper's idea that if media have any impact at all it is in the direction of reinforcement.

Selective attention : See selective exposure.

Selective exposure : The idea that people expose themselves or attend to those messages that are consistent with their preexisting attitudes and beliefs.

Selective perception: Idea that people interpret messages in a manner consistent with their preexisting attitudes and beliefs.

Selective processes : People expose themselves to, remember best and longest, and reinterpret messages that are consistent with their preexisting attitudes and beliefs.

Selective retention : Assumes that people remember best and longest those messages that are consistent with their existing attitudes and beliefs.

Signs	:	In social construction of reality, things that have subjective meaning in social construction of reality, things that have subjective meaning.
Social cognitive theory	:	The idea that people learn by observation.
Social construction of reality	:	Theory for explaining how cultures construct and maintain their realities using signs and symbols; argues that people learn to behave in their social world through interaction with it.
Symbolic interaction	:	The idea that people give meaning to symbols and then those symbols control peoples' behavior in their presence
Symbols	:	In social construction of reality, things that have objective meaning.
Two-step flow theory	:	The idea that mediaís influence on peopleís behavior is limited by opinion leaders, people who initially consume media content, interpret it in light of their own values and beliefs, and then pass it on to opinion followers†who have less frequent contact with media.
Typification schemes	:	In social construction of reality, collections of meanings people have assigned to some phenomenon or situation.

Uses and gratifications approach : The idea that media don't do things to people; people do things with media.

Browsers : Software programs that translate HTML code to allow users to view sites on the World Wide Web.

Brush Tool : A Photoshop 6 tool used to add color or effects to images.

Brushes Palette : A Photoshop window that displays the different sizes and styles available for the paintbrush tool.

Cell : The intersection of a row and a column in a table or spreadsheet into which data can be input.

Clone Tool : A Photoshop tool, located on the Tools palette, which can copy part of an image and reproduce it in the same photo.

CMYK : A color scheme commonly used for full-color printed images, reflecting cyan, magenta, yellow and black inks that combine to form the images on a four-color press.

Codec : An electronic method that converts analog signals, such as video and voice signals, into digital form while also compressing file sizes. It is an acronym for coder-decoder.

Color Separations : The black and white printed equivalent of each color variant within the CMYK color scheme, used to create templates printing each color separately on a four-color press.

Cropping : The process of cutting elements out of a photo.

Cut : In video editing, a quick transition from one clip to the next characterized by no special effect.

Database-driven sites : Database-driven sites require headings that can be read by a program as categories of information, which are then used for sorting the information in those categories. An example is a site with a catalog; orders and inventory information are kept in a database.

Digital Camera : A photographic device used to record images without the use of film.

Digital Noise : Enlarged pixels or extra bits of digital data scattered throughout a photo. Often a result of enlarging a photo with relatively few pixels to begin with.

Downloading : The process of retrieving a computer file from a remote location and placing it on a local computer, usually via the Internet.

Eyedropper Tool : A Photoshop tool that allows user to pick a color from within an image, in addition to colors available in the Photoshop color palettes.

Filters : Tools that can change the look of an image by screening out or applying different effects.

FireWire : A hardware link between an Apple computer and an input device such as an external hard drive or video camera.

Flatbed Scanners : Devices used for importing two-dimensional art and other work, such as printed photos, into a digital image program.

Forms : A web page element that uses database fields and tools in its design to solicit information from visitors to a web site.

Frames : A layout structure for the web in which two or more individual web pages are displayed at once on the same monitor screen.

GIF : One of two file types used for Web publications, GIF files use only 256 colors in their images and have larger file sizes. GIFs also can be animated for publication on the Web.

History Palette : A floating window that keeps track of all steps taken in Photoshop. Users can undo any step by dragging it to the trashcan in the History palette.

HTML	:	Hypertext Markup Language is the computer code written to make web pages work.
Hyperlinks	:	A word or graphic area that, when activated, transports a web site visitor to another place on the World Wide Web.
Input	:	The process of bringing raw material into a computer program, usually with the purpose of molding it into a finished product.
JPEG	:	The other file type used for Web publications. Even though JPEG file sizes are generally smaller than GIF files, JPEG files can use more than 1,000 colors and are most often used for reproducing photographic images on the Web.
Lasso Tool	:	A Photoshop tool that allows users to select small parts of individual photos, wrapping to each edge of that part.
NAT	:	The abbreviation used in shooting scripts for natural sound, or sound that is recorded through the regular course of shooting.
Navigation Bar	:	A list of links found at the top, bottom or left of a web page that allow visitors to find any page within a given web site.
Output	:	The process of sending a finished product from a program

to its final resting place, such as a disk, printed hard copy, or Web destination.

Paintbrush tool : A Photoshop tool used to add color and effects to images by smoothing them on with strokes in a variety of sizes and widths.

Pixels : The small dots that make up an electronic image; equivalent in memory to a bit.

Post-production : The period after taping in which a final video project is produced and edited

Producers : People who produce a video from raw footage, both audio and video.

PSD : Stands for Photoshop Document; this file type is limited to use within the Photoshop program.

Resampling : The process of changing the pixel dimensions in an electronic photo to adjust image size.

RGB : A color scheme commonly used for electronic images, reflecting red, green and blue pixel color combinations.

A GLOSSARY OF MEDIA LITERACY TERMS

Broadcasting : Producing and designing media content to appeal to a broad audience segment and offered on airways to a large number of people. The technology of broadcasting only applies to content carried through the airwaves.

Cablecasting : The delivery of media content through underground or overhead cables. Refers to the technology of cable. Content production and design resembles narrowcasting.

Face-to-Face Communication : The sender and receiver of information are in direct contact. The receiver may disagree, ask a question, or repeat information. The sender and receiver can engage in a dialogue about the message.

Feedback : The process of communication whereby a person can disagree, ask a question, repeat information for understanding, or otherwise talk back in the communication process.

Gatekeepers : Those in control of the flow of information. The gatekeeper can choose to make available or withhold information for public consumption. Newspaper publishers, editors and reporters, television producers, radio station owners and broadcasting executives have all been cited as examples of media gatekeepers.

Genre : Specific kinds of media content, e.g. drama, comedy, situation comedy, talk shows, news, advertising, cartoons, etc. On Channels 45/49, we broadcast several genres: how-to programs, drama, public affairs, children's programs, British comedies, documentaries, travelogues, etc. Each genre has its own general purpose and design.

Mass Media : Any form of communication produced by a few people for the consumption by many people. Mass media are channels of communication through which messages flow. As the messages go through the channels, they are distorted. When people receive media messages they have no opportunity for immediate feedback with the producers of the messages.

Media : Any physical object used to communicate. Common media are televisions, radios, telephones and newspapers. Media also extend to building materials, paint, sculpture, dance and other conventions for communicating ideas. Singular form of media is medium.

Media Content : Messages which are produced by the few for the many and delivered to large audiences simultaneously.

Media Languages : Media conventions, formats, symbols and narrative structures that cue the audience to meaning. The symbolic language of electronic media works much the same way as grammar works in print media.

Media Literacy : The ability to read, analyze, evaluate and produce communication in a variety of media forms (television, print, radio, computers, etc.).

Media Technology : The hardware used to create information and communicate it, such as radio, computers, telephones, satellites, printing presses, pencils, etc.

Media Use : The way people interact with media. The use of media varies from person to person, group to group and at various times during an individual's life.

Medium Singular for media : Television is a mass medium. Radios, televisions and newspapers are mass media.

Narrowcasting : Producing and designing media content in order to target a highly specific segment of the population. Opposite of broadcasting.

Objective : The ideal that the media producer is representing a balanced viewpoint on issues. The ideal that media producers are fair and accurate conduits for information. Opposite of subjective.

Representation : The relationship between actual places, people, events and ideas and media content. Stereotypes are a common form of media representation.

Target Audience : A group of people within a population that the media agency would like to reach. For instance, the "target audience" for PBS's children's programming isn't "everyone"--it's young children and their parents or caregivers. Just as common are the audiences targeted, sold and delivered to advertisers by media agencies. Groups are targeted on the basis of demographics (age, ethnicity, level of education, income, etc.), media use patterns, zip codes and other factors.

Adjacency : An advertising pod positioned next to a particular TV or radio program. Also called commercial break positions.

Affidavit : A statement, usually notarized, accompanying station invoices which confirms that the commercial actually ran at the time stated on the invoice.

Affiliate : A station associated with a network by contract to broadcast the network's programs.

Air Date : The first broadcast of a commercial; also refers to the exact date of a particular TV or radio program.

Audilog : The diary used by household members in Nielsen's local rating sample which records what stations and programs they viewed during a week's time.

Audimeter : Nielsen's device for electronically recording TV viewing in sample households. Has been replaced nationally by the People Meter, but still being used in selected markets.

Availability ("avails") : Unsold units of time available for broadcasters to sell to advertisers. Also refers to a station's submission of programs and rating estimates for advertising planning and buying.

Average Quarter-Hour Rating : The audience estimate reported by Nielsen and Arbitron for television and radio. It provides the average number of persons or households who watched/ listened for at least 5 minutes of the 15 minute segment being reported.

Bonus Spot : Additional TV or radio spot provided to an advertiser at no charge to raise the overall audience delivery of the schedule.

Break Position : A broadcast commercial aired between two programs instead of in the middle of one program.

Broadcast Calendar : An industry-accepted calendar used mainly for accounting and billing purposes. Weeks run Monday-Sunday, and each month is four or five weeks long.

Cable TV : TV programming that is delivered by coaxial cable rather than over the air for the purposes of improved reception and delivery of additional program choices beyond the local stations.

Clearance : A station's agreement to carry a particular program.

Cut-In : A commercial inserted by the local station that covers the commercial airing at the same time on the network at the advertiser's request. Useful for testing different copy in a limited geography.

Daypart : One of the time segments into which the day is divided by broadcast media, determined by type of programming and who provides it (network or local).

Designated Market Area (DMA) : Nielsen's term for geographical areas made up of exclusive counties based on which home market stations receive the predominant share of viewing.

Diary : An instrument for measuring viewing, listening or reading of media vehicles kept by people in a sample.

Drive Time : the dayparts used in radio to signify primary listening being done in cars. Generally considered to be Monday-Friday 6- 10 a.m. and 3-7 p.m. HUT-(Households Using Television) - a broadcast research term indicating the percent of homes with sets on during a specific time period.

ID : Station identification of its call letters and location, channel or frequency. Also refers to any commercial message less than ten seconds long.

Infomercial : A long (more than two minutes) commercial providing extensive product/service description and sales information.

Log : Chronological record of a station's program and commercial exact air times.

Network : Two or more stations joined by a line to broadcast the same program from a few original studios simultaneously.

Network Affiliate : A television or radio station that designates a portion of its air time for network programs.

O & O Station	:	A station owned and operated by a network.
O.T.O.	:	One time only, usually referring to a TV or radio special program.
Overnights	:	Audience data provided by Nielsen or Arbitron to metered market clients the day after the broadcast.
Pay Per View	:	A type of Pay TV where viewers are charged each time they watch the special event or movie being broadcast.
Pay TV	:	A TV system providing programs which are available only to the households who subscribe, usually transmitted via coaxial cable or telephone lines. Also called "premium channels" on cable, such is HBO, Cinemax, Showtime, Disney Channel, etc.
Persons Using Radio (PUR)	:	The percent of the area's population listening to radio at a specific time.
Piggyback	:	Back-to-back scheduling of two or more brand commercials of one advertiser in network or spot positions.
Pilot	:	A sample of a proposed television series.
Pocketpiece	:	Nielsen's weekly reports providing audience estimates for all network and syndicated programs.

Pre-emption : The substitution of one advertiser's local TV commercial by another advertiser paying a higher price for the spot, or by a different program of interest.

PVT/PUT (Persons Viewing or Using Television) : The percent of individuals viewing all television stations during a specific time period, indicating total viewing to TV in general, not to a specific program or station.

Roadblocking : A scheduling technique where a brand's commercial airs at approximately the same time on all three networks or on all stations in a given market.

R.O.S. (Run Of Schedule or Run Of Station) : A broadcast schedule, similar to R.O.P. where specific programs and air times have not been requested by the advertiser.

Simulcast : Broadcast of the same program at the same time on both AM and FM radio stations. Can also refer to a radio station simultaneously broadcasting the audio portion of a TV program.

Spill-In : The amount of programming viewed within a market area to stations that are licensed to an adjacent market.

Spill-Out : The amount of viewing to local stations outside the home market area.

Strip : A program scheduled at the same time each day, typically Monday-Friday.

Superstation : An independent station whose signal is transmitted to many markets via a satellite.

Sweeps : The four 4-week periods when all TV markets are measured by Nielsen and Arbitron for station viewing and demographic information. Sweep months are February, May, July and November.

Syndicated Program : A program bought by a station or advertiser from an independent organization, not a network.

TAP (Total Audience Plan) : A radio schedule consisting of equal distribution of commercials across all major dayparts.

Turnover : The ratio of a cumulative audience to the average audience for a given period of time. Indicates how loyal a given audience may be for specific stations or programs.

Upfront : A term indicating that an advertiser has purchased advertising for the coming broadcast year in an early buying season, typically for the benefit of lower rates and CPM guarantees.

GENERAL MEDIA TERMS

Advertising Impressions : The audience delivery of media vehicles, programs or schedules. Usually expressed as thousands (000).

Advertising Research Foundation (ARF) : A non-profit organization of advertisers, agencies and the media for promoting advertising effectiveness through objective research.

Advertising Weight : The level of advertising support over a period of time, expressed in gross rating points, impressions, target audience reached, etc.

Aided Recall : A research technique where the respondent is given aid to help remember all or parts of advertising.

As It Falls : A testing method whereby the media test market receives the same media weight, purchased locally, as it would receive from a national theoretical plan.

Average Frequency : The number of times the average person or household is exposed to an advertising schedule. It is always derived from Gross Rating Points and Reach.

Barter : A term used to indicate that advertising was paid for by the advertiser using goods and services rather than cash.

BDI (Brand Development Index) : A measure of the strength of a brand's sales in a particular geographic area indexed to the national sales average.

CDI (Category Development Index) : A measurement of a brand's sales potential using sales of all brands within a category in a specific market indexed to national sales average.

Clutter : The term given to the proliferation of advertising messages aimed at consumers. In TV, it refers to all nonprogram minutes, such as commercials, station promo-tions, billboards, public service announcements, etc.

Cost Per Rating Point (Cost Per Point, CPP, Cost Per GRP) : The cost to reach one percent of the universe, households or individuals, in a given market or geographic area.

Cost Per Thousand (CPM) : The cost to reach 1,000 units of audience, households or individuals, for advertising. Used as a measure of efficiency among media and media schedules.

Coverage Area : The specific geography where a media vehicle has its coverage. In broadcast, coverage usually describes the area to which the station's signal extends. In print, coverage usually means the circulation area.

Cume (Cumulative Audience) : Another way of expressing reach. The total number of different people or households exposed to advertising at least once during the media schedule.

Direct Response Advertising : Any advertising message that calls for a prompt response to purchase a product or request more information.

Duplication : The number or percent of the target audience in one media vehicle also exposed to another vehicle.

Efficiency : The ratio of cost to size of audience used to compare media vehicles, plans or schedules.

Exclusivity : An agreement whereby a media vehicle agrees to run no advertising directly competitive to the advertiser purchasing the media vehicle or program.

First Refusal : The opportunity for an advertiser to extend sponsorship rights of a program or vehicle before it is offered to another advertiser.

Fixed Position : An advertising position which remains fixed over time, such as the inside cover of a magazine.

Flighting : A technique for extending advertising dollars using periods of media activity interspersed with periods of inactivity.

Flow Chart	:	A calendar which dimensionalizes media activity over time, usually a year.
FY	:	An abbreviation for Fiscal Year.
Gross Impressions	:	The combined audiences of several media vehicles or several announcements within a vehicle, leaving in the duplication among the audiences.
Gross Rating Points (GRP's)	:	The sum of individual ratings in a media plan.
Guarantee	:	A commitment to the advertiser by a medium that should audience delivery fall short of what was estimated, the advertiser will receive bonus advertising to meet the expected CPM or GRP's.
Heavy-up	:	An increase in advertising activity for a limited period of time.
Hiatus	:	A scheduled period of inactivity between advertising flights.
Little America (or Little U.S.)	:	Refers to the method of media testing where a national campaign might be tested first in markets that are most similar demographically to the total country.
LNA (Leading National Advertisers)	:	A syndicated research source reporting advertisers' spending in media: network and spot TV, network radio, magazines,

		newspaper supplements and outdoor.
Mail-Order Advertising	:	Type of advertising in which the complete sales transaction takes place through the mail.
Makegood	:	Comparable unit of advertising offered at no charge when the original spot or ad did not run or ran incorrectly.
Mediamark Research Inc. (MRI)	:	A syndicated research source measuring print and broadcast media audiences and product/ brand usage profiles.
Net Cost	:	Advertising rates which do not include advertising agency commission and/or include discounts.
Penetration	:	The degree to which a medium or vehicle has coverage in a specific area. Can also refer to the effectiveness of advertising's impact on consumers.
Per Inquiry (P.I.)	:	Agreement between a media owner and an advertiser where the advertiser pays the owner for advertising on the basis of the number of inquiries or completed sales from the advertising.
Psychographic	:	Describes consumers on the basis of some psychological trait, characteristics or life style.
Quintile	:	The division of the audience or sample into five equal groups ranging from heaviest to lightest

		amount of exposure to any medium.
Rate Card	:	A statement by a medium showing advertising costs, issue dates, program names, closing dates, requirements, cancellation dates, etc.
Rating	:	An estimate of the size of an audience expressed as one percent of the total population.
Reach	:	The unduplicated percent of a potential audience exposed to advertising one or more times during a given period.
Roll Out	:	An advertising technique where advertising is expanded to cover more and more markets as distribution/ product sales are also expanded.
Share	:	The percent of an audience tuned to a particular program at a given time.
Share of Voice (SOV)	:	A brand's percent of the total advertising weight in its product category.
Short Rate	:	The cost difference between the discounted contract rate and the higher rate actually earned by an advertiser if he fails to fulfill the contracted amount of advertising.
Simmons Market Research Bureau (SMRB)	:	A syndicated source of print and broadcast audience measurement, as well as product usage data.

Sponsorship : Purchase of all or part of a TV program or all pages of a magazine.

Standard Rate & Data Service (SRDS) : Monthly reports of publications', TV and radio stations' rate cards and supporting technical information arranged by state and market.

Starch : A research company providing print advertising readership information.

Telmar : A computer system offering various media planning systems for reach and frequency, as well as cross tabulation of data from Simmons and MRI.

Vehicle : Anything capable of exposing advertising to customers.

INTERNET MEDIA TERMS

Bookmark : A routine that allows you to save a reference to a site or page that you have already visited. At a later point in time, you can use a bookmark to return to that page. It commonly refers to a feature of Netscape Navigator (a web browser) that allows you to collect and organize bookmarks of your favorite web sites.

Browser : An application used to view and navigate the World Wide Web and other Internet resources.

Browser war : A catch phrase that refers to the battles between Netscape and Microsoft for dominance of the web browser market. Both sides seek to maximize their product's marketshare and mindshare in cyberspace. The battles are marked by short product development cycles, publicity campaigns, provocative public statements, appeals for federal intervention, and a general desire to crush the other side.

Bug : Problem with computer software or hardware that causes it to malfunction or crash.

Bulletin Board System (BBS) : An open computer system that members can dial into in order to send email, join discussion groups, and download files. Since the 1970s, BBS's have provided an early means for home users to get online. Originally, BBS's were free-standing local systems, but now many provide access to Internet email, telnet, FTP, and other Internet services.

Chat : A form of interactive online communication that enables typed conversations to occur in real-time. When participating in a chat discussion, your messages are instantaneously relayed to other members in the chat room while other members' messages are instantaneously relayed to you.

Chat jistory : A transcript of a chat session.

Commercial Online Service : A computer network that supplies its members with access to chat rooms, bulletin boards, and other online content on a monthly fee basis. Commercial online services include America Online, CompuServe, The Microsoft Network, and Prodigy. In addition to their own proprietary content, most commercial online services also provide access to the Internet.

Congestion : A state occurring in a part of a network when the message traffic is so heavy that it slows down network response time.

Connection : When two computers have established a path through which the exchange of information can occur.

Cookies : Small files that are downloaded to your computer when you browse certain web pages. Cookies hold information that can be retrieved by other web pages on the site. Some cookies are programmed with an expiration date so that they are automatically deleted after a period of time.

Copy protection : A software lock placed on a computer program by its developer to thwart piracy. This preventative measure was widely used in the mid-1980s but later abandoned by many developers because of numerous customer complaints.

Cracker : A malicious hacker who breaks (or cracks) the security of computer systems in order to access, steal, or destroy sensitive information. "Hacker" is often incorrectly used instead of cracker, especially by the media. See also hacker.

Crossload : To send an attached file via email. See also upload and download.

Domain name : The official name of a computer connected to the Internet. Domain names are derived from a hierarchical system, with a host name followed by a top-level domain category. The top-level domain categories are com (for commercial enterprises), org (for non-profit organizations), net (for network services providers), mil (for the military), and gov (for government).

Domain Name System (DNS) : A database system which looks up host IP addresses based upon domain names. For example if you ask for "www.thisismyhost.com" it will return 123.45.67.89. Copies of the Domain Name System are distributed through the Internet.

Download : To transfer data from a larger "host" system to a smaller "client" system's hard drive or other local storage device. See also upload.

Download charges : Monetary charges associated with downloading a file from a commercial online service. This method of information exchange is not very popular.

Ecash : Electronic money designed to be used over a network or stored on cards similar to credit cards. Ecash is still more of an idea than a practical reality, largely due to security concerns.

Eform : An electronic form that is filled out by a user and sent over a network. They are typically used to place orders or provide feedback. Eforms can be placed on web pages or in Java applets and usually contain text boxes, buttons, and other components.

Emoticon : A cute sideways face created by using special characters on the keyboard. Used to express emotions without words. For example, this winking face ;-) indicates "I'm joking", this sad face :-(expresses sadness or "I'm sulking". If this makes no sense, turn your head sideways and look again. Also known as a "smiley".

Encryption : A procedure that renders the contents of a message or file unintelligible to anyone not authorized to read it. PGP (Pretty Good Privacy) is a commonly-used encryption program.

Eyeballs : A viewing audience for a WWW site.

Facilitated chat : In a facilitated chat, a host or facilitator controls the messages that appear on the chat screen. Usually used when there is a guest speaker. Facilitated chats provide an orderly environment for the guest speaker and ensure that she is not overwhelmed with dozens of questions all being asked at once. See also chat.

FAQ : Acronym for Frequently Asked Questions. A reference document created for particular topic or group that answers to common beginners' questions. It is considered poor Netiquette to ask a question without first reading the FAQ.

Flame : A public post or email message that expresses a strong opinion or criticism. Flames can be fun when they allow people to vent their feelings, then return to the topic at hand. Others are simply insulting and can lead to flame wars.

Flame Bait : An inflammatory post that is designed to provoke a flame war or flame responses.

Flame on/Flame off : Notifiers that surround a flame message and let readers know that the message they are reading is a flame. Although you don't see these as much as you used to, they would most commonly be used by an individual known to a particular online group who wishes to do a little ranting and then return to the topic at hand. Note that the original usage of "flame on" was derived from Marvel Comics' Human Torch character.

Flame war : A series of public posts in which people flame one another rather than contribute useful information.

Flash session : A feature of America Online that automatically performs online tasks at a designated time. Flash sessions are often used to send/receive email and download large files.

Forum : A topically-focused discussion

group or area. From the traditional Roman forum.

Go word : The word associated with a forum or area on a commercial online service that allows you to get to that place quickly.

Hacker : An expert programmer who likes to spend a lot of time figuring out the finer details of computer systems or networks, as opposed to those who learn only the minimum necessary. See also cracker.

Handle : A nickname used in online communications.

Hit : A single user accessing a single file from a web server. A unit of measure often used erroneously to evaluate the popularity of a web site.

Home page : A web page that is topically the main source of information about a particular person, group, or concept. Many people on the web create home pages about themselves for fun; these are also known as vanity pages.

Host : 1. A computer that allows users to communicate with other host computers on a network.

2. A chat term for someone who is managing a chat. Hosts often act as referees and have the power to turn participants into spectators and vice-versa.

Hyperlink : A highlighted word or picture within a hypertext document that when clicked takes you to another place within the document or to another document altogether.

Hypertext : Text that includes links or shortcuts to other documents, allowing the reader to easily jump from one text to related texts, and conse-quentially from one idea to another, in a non-linear fashion. Coined by Ted Nelson in 1965.

Hypertext Markup Language (HTML) : The tag-based ASCII language used to create pages on the World Wide Web. See also hypertext.

Hypertext Transfer Protocol (HTTP): : The protocol used by the World Wide Web to transfer HTML files.

Icon : A small graphic image that represents a file or application and when clicked upon produces a programmed result. Use of this mnemonic convention originated at Xerox PARC and was subsequently popularized by the Apple Macintosh. Producing an effective icon is non-trivial because of size and color restraints. See iconographer.

Iconographe : A skillful designer who elevates icon design to an art form.

Identity Hacking : Posing as someone else. Posting anonymously or pseudonymously, usually with the intent to deceive.

Infobahn : A variant of information superhighway. An unimplemented proposal by Vice President Al Gore to wire the US for hundreds of cable television channels. Now synonymous with the Internet.

Integrated Services Digital Network (ISDN) : A technology offered by telephone carriers that allows for the rapid transfer of voice and data.

Internet : A worldwide network of networks that all use the TCP/ IP communications protocol and share a common address space. First incarnated as the ARPANET in 1969, the Internet has metamorphosed from a military internetwork to an academic research internetwork to the current commercial internetwork. It commonly supports services such as email, the World Wide Web, file transfer, and Internet Relay Chat. The Internet is experiencing tremendous growth in the number of users, hosts, and domain names. It is gradually subsuming other media, such as proprietary computer networks, newspapers, books, television, and the telephone. Also known as "the net", "the information superhighway", and "cyber-space". See also domain, and Domain Name Service.

Internet explorer : A free web browser application from Microsoft.

Internet Relay Chat (IRC) : A chat network that operates over the Internet. Originally evolved from the UNIX talk program, IRC is similar to the chat systems found on commercial online services.

Internet Service Provider (ISP) : 1. A business that delivers access to the Internet, usually for a monthly fee. PSI, UUNET, and Netcom are examples of established ISPs but there are thousands of smaller ones all around the world.

2. Any business that provides Internet services such as web sites or web site development.

Internet Society (ISOC) : To quote its home page at http: /info.isoc.org: "The Internet Society is a non-governmental International organization for global cooperation and coordination for the Internet and its internetworking technologies and applications."

InterNIC : The InterNIC is the entity that controls the registration of most domain names on the Internet. The InterNIC is a cooperative activity between the National Science Foundation, Network Solutions, Inc. and AT&T. Its home page is at http://internic.net/

Interoperability : The ability of software and hardware on multiple machines from multiple vendors to communicate meaningfully.

Intranet : A private network that uses Internet-related technologies to provide services within an organization.

IP address : A string of four numbers separated by periods (such as 111.22.3.444) used to represent a computer on the Internet. The format of the address is specified by the Internet Protocol in RFC 791. When a PC accesses the Internet through an ISP, it sometimes receives a temporary IP address.

Jack In : To log in to a machine or connect to a network. Derived from cyberpunk fiction.

Java : An object oriented programming language created by Sun Microsystems. Java is a device independent language, meaning that programs compiled in Java can be run on any computer. Java programs can be run as a free-standing application or as an applet placed on a web page. Applets written in Java are served from a web site but executed on the client computer. Java applets have a built-in security feature which prevents them from accessing the file system of the client computer. See also applet. Here is the Java version of "Hello World!": class HelloWorld {public static void main (String args[]) {System. out.println("Hello World!"); }}

JavaScript : A scripting language that allows lines of Java code to be inserted into HTML scripts.

Joint Photographic Experts Group (JPEG) : An image compression standard for still photographs that is commonly used on the web.

Kermit : A protocol used for transferring files over a dial-up connection that is commonly used on BBS systems.

Kill File : A file used by some USENET reading programs that filters out unwanted messages, usually from a particular author or on a particular subject. If you add someone to your kill file, you arrange for the person to be ignored by your news reader.

Leased Line : a permanently established connection between computers over a dedicated phone line which is leased from a telephone carrier.

Line Noise : Static over a telephone line that interferes with network communications.

Link : A highlighted word or picture within a hypertext document that when clicked bring you to another place within the document or to another document altogether. See also hyperlink.

List Server : An automated mailing list distribution system. List servers maintain a list of email addresses to be used for mass emailing. Subscribing and unsubscribing to the list is accomplished by sending a properly formatted email message to the list server.

Local Area Network: (LAN) A group of computers at a single location (usually an office or home) that are connected by phone lines or coaxial cable.

Mailbomb : The act of sending massive amounts of email to a single address with the malicious intent of disrupting the system of the recipient. Mailbombing is considered a serious breach of Netiquette and is probably illegal.

Mailing List : A discussion group that occurs via mass email distributions.

Mailing lists are usually maintained by individuals utilizing list server software. List servers maintain a list of email addresses to be used for the mailing list. Subscribing and unsubscribing to the list is accomplished by sending a properly formatted email message to the list server.

Mirror Site : A server which contains a duplicate of another WWW or FTP site. Mirror sites are created when the traffic on the original site becomes too heavy for a single server. Often mirror sites are located in different geographic areas allowing users to choose the site closest to them.

Nanosecond : A measurement of time. There are 1,000,000,000 nanoseconds in a second.

Navigator : A web browser application from Netscape.

Net Lingo : The slang commonly used on the Internet.net.police. Those who feel it's their appointed role to flame perceived violations of Netiquette.

Net Surfing : Browsing or exploring a network or the World Wide Web to find places of interest, usually without a specific goal in mind. Analogous to channel surfing with a TV remote control.

Netiquette : Network etiquette, or the set of informal rules of behavior that have evolved in Cyberspace, including the Internet and online services.

Netlag : A condition that occurs on the Internet in which response time is greatly slowed due to heavy traffic.

Netnews : The content of USENET.

Network : A group of computers or devices that are connected together for the exchange of data and sharing of resources.

Newsgroup : A public place where messages are posted for public consumption and response. The most available distribution of newsgroups is USENET which contains over ten thousand unique newsgroups covering practically every human proclivity. The names of newsgroups are comprised of a string of words separated by periods, such as "rec.humor. funny" or "misc.jobs. offered". The first word (i.e. "rec" or "misc") represents the top level category of newsgroups. The second word (in these examples "humor" and "jobs") represents a subcategory of the first level, and the third word a subcategory of the second.

Non-Disclosure Agreement (NDA) : A contract commonly used by computer companies to protect the confidentiality of unreleased products. Software developers, reporters, and sometimes beta testers are often required to sign these before they are given access to either information about upcoming products or the product itself.

Offline : 1. As an adjective, not connected to a computer network.

2. As an adverb, not here or not now, as in "Let's take this discussion offline." Often used to indicate that a topic should be discussed privately rather than in a public forum.

Online : 1. Currently connected to a host, opposite of offline.

2. Referring to anything connected to a computer network.

Password : A secret code that you utilize along with your user ID in order to log on to a network.

Path : The hierarchical description of where a directory, folder, or file is located on your computer or on a network

Post : To send a message to a public area like a BBS or newsgroup where it can be read by many others.

Postmaster	:	The name given to the person in charge of administrating email for a particular site. According to convention, mail sent to postmaster@foo.com should be read by a real live person. Protocol | A series of rules and conventions that allow different kinds of computers and applications to communicate over a network.
Query	:	1. A general question posed to a person or group over the Internet.Internet users are generally so helpful that if one asks an appropriate query to the correct discussion group, one will often receive many useful responses. One caveat: it is necessary to find and read the appropriate FAQ document first. Failure to do so would be considered a waste other people's time and bandwidth. 2. A request for specific information from a database.
Random Access Memory (RAM)	:	The working memory of the computer into which application programs can be loaded and executed. It helps to have more of this "working space" installed when running advanced operating systems and applications.
README File	:	1. A text file included with an application that contains

important (and often last minute) information about installing and using the application.

2. A text file on an FTP site that provides valuable information about the context of site.

3. Any text file that you are supposed to read before proceeding.

Read Receipts : An optional email feature that notifies you when a recipient has opened the email message you sent him. See also delivery receipts.

Refresh : To clear the screen or part of the screen and redraw it again.

Remote Login : Operating a remote computer over a network as if it were a local computer. This can be accomplished via one of several protocols, including telnet and the UNIX program rlogin.

Response Time : A measurement of the time between a request for information over a network and the network's fulfillment of that request. "Overall response time" is an aggregate or average measurement of various response times over a particular network or through a particular host.

Search Engine : A program or web site that enables users to search for keywords on web pages throughout the World Wide Web. For example, Alta Vista is a popular search engine located at http://www.altavista.com/

Security : Ensuring that private information remains private in an atmosphere where all other information is free. Security also means that viruses are prevented from infecting people's systems.

Server : A computer that provides information to client machines. For example, there are web servers that send out web pages, mail servers that deliver email, list servers that administer mailing lists, FTP servers that hold FTP sites and deliver files to users who request them, and name servers that provide information about Internet host names.

Shareware : Software that you can download from a network and "try before you buy." If you like the software and decide to use it beyond the trial period, you must register with the author and pay a registration fee.

Shouting : Typing In All Capital Letters Is Considered Shouting In Online Communications. Avoid this unless you really mean to shout.

Snail Mail : Regular postal mail, as opposed to email. Pejorative when implying postal mail's slowness relative to email.

Sneakernet : The transfer of electronic information by physically carrying disks, tape, or some other media from one machine to another. Used ironically.

Spam : To send a message (usually an advertisement) to many discussion groups (bulletin boards, mailing lists, and/or newsgroups), without regard for its topical relevance.

Telecommunications: The science of sending signals representing voice, video, or data through telephone lines.

Telecommuting : To work at home and use a computer and modem to communicate with the office.

Telnet : A protocol which allows you to sign onto a remote UNIX computer from a another computer located anywhere on the Internet. To telnet into a remote computer, you usually need to supply a user ID and password that is recognized by the remote system.

Thread : (1) A series of postings on a particular topic. Threads can be a series of bulletin board messages (for example, when someone posts a question and others reply with answers or additional queries on the same topic). A thread can also apply to chats, where multiple conversation threads may exist simultaneously.

(2) Also refers to an independent process taking place in a multitasking environment.

Toggle : 1. A switch that is either on or off.

2. If it is on, to turn it off; if it is off, to turn it on.

Traffic : The load of packets carried by a network or portion of a network. Heavy traffic slows down the response time of the individual packets.

Triple-dub : An abbreviated way to say "WWW" when reciting a URL.

Upload : To send a file to a network. See also download and crossload.

Virtual : A commonly used adjective that means having all of the properties of x while not necessarily being x. For example, "virtual Friday" in a workplace is the last day of work before a break, that is to say it is like Friday but may or may not actually be Friday. A "virtual reality" is an artificial environment that appears to be its own reality. On a mainframe, a "virtual machine" gives the user all of the properties and "feel" of a separate personal computer.

Virus : An insidious piece of computer code written to damage systems. Viruses can be hidden in executable program files posted online.

Webliography : A listing of source World Wide Web sites.

Webmaster : The person in charge of administrating a World Wide Web site. By convention, the webmaster of Internet domain foo.com can be reached at the email address webmaster @foo.com.

World Wide Web (WWW) : A distributed hypertext system invented by Tim Berners-Lee on a NeXT Computer. Currently, one of the most popular services offered on the Internet. Web pages are viewed using browsing software like Netscape Navigator, Sun Microsystems Hot Java, or Microsoft Internet Explorer. See also browser, Hypertext Markup Language, net surfing, and triple-dub.

Worm : (1) An insidious and usually illegal computer program that is designed to replicate itself over a network for the purpose of causing harm and/or destruction. While a virus is designed to invade a single computer's hard drive, a worm is designed to invade a network. The most infamous worm was created by Robert Tappan Morris in November 1988; it infiltrated over 6,000 network systems around the globe.

(2) Acronym for "Write Once Read Many". Used to describe optical disk drives that can only be written once, usually for archival purposes.

OUT-OF-HOME TERMS

Billboard : An outdoor advertising display. Also, in broadcast, a short 5 or 10 second announcement indicating advertiser sponsorship of a program.

Facing : In outdoor, the number of billboards at a location facing in the same direction. In marketing, the number of units facing the shopper on a shelf in a grocery, drug, discount store. etc.

Poster Panel : The standard outdoor advertising display unit, usually 25' × 12'.

Showing : A group of outdoor boards which provide a certain percent coverage of a market, usually purchased in increments of 25 (e.g. a #25 showing, a #50 showing, a #75 showing, a #100 showing).

PRINT MEDIA TERMS

Article : A story based on the facts.

Audit Bureau of Circulations (ABC) : Organization of publishers, advertising agencies and advertisers for verifying the circulation statements of member publications.

Advertising Checking Bureau (ACB) : A company which provides advertisers and agencies with newspaper tear sheets of ads which have run.

Agate Line : A unit of measurement for newspaper advertising which measures one column wide with 14 agate lines per inch.

Bias : When an editor or reporter expresses a personal point of view in a news article in a series of articles.

Bleed : A term used for print advertising that extends all the way to the edge of the page with no margin. Many magazines charge a premium for the bleed, usually 15%.

Business Publication: Audit of Circulation (BPA) An organization for auditing the circulation of business (trade) publications.

Checkerboard . Magazine advertising that uses diagonal quarter or half page ads alternating with editorial.

Checking Copy : A copy of a publication sent to the advertiser and the agency as proof the ad ran as ordered.

Circulation : The total number of distributed copies of a publication at a specified time. Also, in broadcast, the total number of households within the station's coverage area. In outdoor, the number of people passing the billboards who have an opportunity to see the advertising.

Closing Date : The date by which all advertising must be ordered from the specific media vehicle in order to secure the dates/ times/positions requested.

Column Inch : A unit of newspaper space one column wide and one inch deep (14 agate lines).

Caption A sentence or phrase under a picture to identify or describe the picture.

Column : A regular article or feature in a newspaper or magazine.

Columnist : A person who writes a regular (daily or weekly) article for a newspaper or magazine, such as a political columnist or a sports columnist.

Credible	:	Believable; worthy of belief or confidence; trustworthy.
Correspondent	:	A person employed by a news organization to gather, report, or contribute news, articles, etc., regularly from a distant place.
Direct Mail Advertising	:	Any printed material sent through the mail directly to prospective customers.
Double Truck	:	A newspaper ad unit that uses two facing full pages, including the gutter or fold.
Editor	:	The head of a news organization; person who chooses the articles that will be printed each day.
Editorial	:	Article written by the editor giving his opinion on a problem or event.
Ethical	:	Pertaining to or dealing with morals; pertaining to right and wrong in conduct.
Eyewitness	:	A person who sees an occurrence with his own eyes and is able to give a firsthand account of it.
Feature	:	A special or regular article, usually displayed prominently.
Front Page	:	The first page of a paper, usually carrying the most important story.
Gutter	:	The blank space between margins of facing pages of a publication.

Headline : Title of any newspaper article.

Journalist : A person who writes articles for a news organization.

Libel : A lie that causes damage (misrepresents damagingly).

Integrity : Soundness or moral character; honesty.

Insertion Order : Written instructions from the advertiser or agency authorizing a publication to run a specific advertisement in a specific issue. Also specifies cost per ad and size of ad, as well as any request for special position in the publication.

Island Position : A print advertisement surrounded completely by editorial.

Line Rate : The cost per agate line for newspapers.

Magazine Supplement : The magazine section of a Sunday newspaper produced either locally or nationally.

Media Vocabulary : Email this article Printer friendly page.

Net Paid Circulation : A term used by ABC for the circulation of a publication for which at least 50% of the subscription or newsstand price has been paid.

News : A report of a recent event; what is reported about a recent event or events.

News Services : News companies that have their own reporters. They sell their articles to the media. Associated Press (AP), United Press International (UPI) and Reuters are the top three news services used in the U.S.

Objective : Not affected by personal feelings or prejudice; based on facts; unbiased.

Ombudsman : A neutral individual employed by a news organization to receive, investigate, report on and (in some instances) resolve reader or viewer complaints against a news organization.

Opinion : What a person thinks about a particular subject; a subjective point of view.

PBW, P4C : Abbreviations for Page Black & White and Page Four Color.

Pass-along Audience: Readers of magazines or newspapers who did not purchase the publication. Also called Secondary Audience.

Publishers Information Bureau (PIB) : A syndicated source of monthly reports on advertising activity in major consumer magazines, reported by product or service category.

Publisher's Statement : A notarized statement from the publisher of total circulation, geographic distribution, method of getting subscriptions, etc.

Plagiarize : To put forth as original to oneself the ideas or words of another.

Readers Per Copy : Average number of readers for one copy of a newspaper or magazine.

Regional Edition : An edition of a national publication's circulation that falls in a certain geographic area for which advertising may be purchased separately, usually at a cost premium.

Remnant Space : Magazine space sold at reduced prices at the last minute when another advertiser's materials do not arrive or to fill out regional editions.

Run of Press or Run of Paper (ROP) : A newspaper insertion for which an exact position is not requested but left to the newspaper's discretion.

Reporter : A person who gathers and reports news for a news organization.

Split Run : Scheduling two or more executions of an advertising message in alternate copies of a magazine's circulation in a given issue.

Source : Someone who gives a reporter information; a supplier of information.

Subjective : Based on personal feelings.

Slander	:	A false report maliciously uttered and tending to injure the reputation of a person.
Story	:	A news article or report.
Tabloid	:	a newspaper measuring about 5-6 columns wide by 200 lines deep, about 2/3 the size of a standard newspaper.
TEAM - Media Buying, Advertising	:	Denver, Colorado All Rights Reserved.
The Media	:	All the means of mass communication (newspapers, TV, radio, websites, magazines).
The Press	:	All the media and agencies that print, broadcast, or gather and transmit news.